403779

D1615369

The
New Rules
of
Business

Leading entrepreneurs reveal their secrets for
success

by Dan Matthews

Hh

HARRIMAN HOUSE LTD

3A Penns Road
Petersfield
Hampshire
GU32 2EW
GREAT BRITAIN

Tel: +44 (0)1730 233870
Fax: +44 (0)1730 233880
Email: enquiries@harriman-house.com
Website: www.harriman-house.com

First published in Great Britain in 2010

Author photo © www.tomoldham.com

Set in Plantin, Clarendon and Clarendon Light

ISBN: 978-1-906659-16-5

British Library Cataloguing in Publication Data
A CIP catalogue record for this book can be obtained from the British Library.

Printed and bound in the UK by CPI Antony Rowe, Chippenham

No responsibility for loss occasioned to any person or corporate body acting or refraining to act as a result of reading material in this book can be accepted by the Publisher, by the Author, or by the employer of the Author.

CONTENTS

THE RULES   **161**

ABOUT THE AUTHOR

Dan Matthews was born in Epsom, Surrey, and educated at Glyn School and Keele University where he achieved a masters degree in global security studies. After a stint as a defence reporter, he  turned to business journalism and since 2001 has held senior editorial positions at some of the UK's biggest newspaper and magazine publishers.

Dan contributes articles to broadsheet newspapers including the *Financial Times* and the *Guardian*, as well as a host of trade titles. In 2008, he set up his own online publishing company dedicated to entrepreneurs. Its first title, LaunchLab.co.uk, launched in November of that year.

Dan is an avid observer of business issues and has made a string of television and radio appearances in the UK. He has interviewed more than 1,000 entrepreneurs, politicians and senior lobbyists, including Gordon Brown, William Hague, Sir Ming Campbell, Sir Stelios Haji-Ioannou, Gordon Ramsay and Peter Jones.

INTRODUCTION

Every year in the UK millions of people don't start a business. Thousands do, but millions do not. Dotted throughout this hefty group are people that don't start businesses because they love what they do already: musicians, artists, actors and millionaire footballers among them. But, these lucky few notwithstanding, most men and women work for a living because they feel they have to and, almost by definition, dread Monday mornings as much as they cherish weekends.

Some readily admit that they gave up resisting becoming a corporate stooge a long time ago – when they weren't selected for trials at Preston North End or when their band failed to break out of the university circuit – while others acknowledge that they are stuck in a cycle of bill-paying that effectively guarantees loyalty to the boss forever.

Once the dreams and ambitions of youth grow dim and as adults we see the folly of our far-fetched goals, it seems we capitulate and give ourselves over to the mundane ravages of the nine-to-five. But this needn't be the case; certainly not since starting a business turned into something that we can all do.

❝I spent time with over 35 leading entrepreneurs. All had important lessons to share. ❞

Becoming an entrepreneur is an attainable third option that has a foot in each of the spheres of wild fantasy and hard work; it gives us a realistic chance to do something special that we love, and get paid for it. Not long ago the concept of starting from scratch and competing with established firms was made real only by people with existing wealth, or by those with exceptional talents and luck. But business has evolved.

The development of phones, computer systems and the internet, the relaxing of regulation and the (fairly new) idea that everyone has an equal opportunity to do well means that there is nothing preventing us from making a fortune, building new products and services and providing employment for others. Little people like you and I are making names for themselves in business all around us, right now.

People think that starting a business is difficult, but it's easy. Making it work is hard, admittedly, but on our side is the simple truth that commerce and endeavour are a part of what it means to be a human being. It's in our blood. Even before the early trading civilisations grew out of the Middle East thousands of years ago we have all been buying at one price and selling at another. The process is no less straightforward now, but for a few extra forms to fill in.

All successful business people have something in common, and it isn't staggering genius: they are able to sell something for more than it costs them to produce it. That's 'Business 101' all wrapped up. No hidden wizardry, no tricks, no secret formulas. You just need a good idea and an efficient way of getting it into the marketplace.

Forget the complexities of the *Financial Times* with its earn-outs, liquidity, reconciliations and accretions. These terms are for accountants and investors, and are mere distractions for the fledgling entrepreneur. You're after sales (money coming in) and profit (the amount left over when all expenses are subtracted from your earnings).

That's why Baron Sugar (Suralan to you and I), who left school before attaining any qualifications, is now worth close to a billion pounds and why Sir Richard Branson, who is famously dyslexic, has been able to launch more successful businesses than you've had hot dinners – as well as the odd dud.

Not everyone I met and profiled in this book sat A Levels, let alone went to university. In fact most got itchy feet while still in their teens and developed a taste for enterprise during those years. Some started with no money and few resources, while others wheeled and dealed until their business grew strong enough to develop exponentially. Some still wheel and deal today.

A few set their sights on entrepreneurial stardom from day one, but many developed their businesses from cottage industries after uncovering demand that they hadn't anticipated. They are surprised by their success, like a bashful movie star accepting an Oscar, and claim that other people's judgement and dedication were responsible for their unexpected eminence.

> **❝ Fortune and sweat are the themes that shape the experience of all entrepreneurs, as are failure and blissful fulfillment. ❞**

When asked why their business flourished, no one in this book said it was exclusively down to their own talents. Everyone admitted they had help and support along the way and most point to the intertwined roles that hard work and potluck played at different times in their journey to eventual success.

Fortune and sweat are themes that shape the experience of all entrepreneurs, as are failure, mistakes, sleepless nights and moments of blissful fulfilment oscillated with dark despair. The secret to entrepreneurial success, if there is one, seems to be perseverance. The truism "the harder I work the luckier I get" was quoted by more than one person profiled in these pages.

With this in mind, the aim of *The New Rules of Business* is to reveal what makes successful entrepreneurs tick: how they started, what helped them develop while others failed and, hard work aside, what special thing or things made their creation transform from a hopeful, tentative start-up to flourishing and admired business.

Their stories are often inspiring, sometimes astonishing, and all shed new light on the practical side of business: why some things work and some don't, how to avoid wrecking a business, what you should do if you make a profit and the best way to react if you, like so many others, fail at the first attempt.

Some of the people interviewed here are billionaires, adorned with accolades and harbouring a lifetime of experiences to draw from.

Others are comparatively new to the game, for whom the first faltering steps of enterprise are still fresh in the memory. Still more are somewhere in-between.

Their demographics – age, ethnicity, gender, location – are varied, as if to prove that no one 'type' of person is more suited to building up businesses than any other. Most, though not all, are millionaires; and at least one of those outside the bracket of 'rich' is there because they choose to be.

Also included is a handful of corporate executives. These captains of industry have responsibility for vast turnovers, gigantic budgets and worldwide brands. While not entrepreneurs – they didn't found the businesses themselves – they are great leaders and are a mine of information about how to deal with people.

If you have bought this book because you are starting up on your own then the author wishes you a bright and rewarding future. The most important advice I can give, having heard all of the magnificent stories of these business leaders in person, is that it's better to try than not to; better to have given your all, than be left wondering what might have been.

Dan Matthews
London, 2010

THE

ENTREPRENEURS

AJAZ AHMED

Intelligent Online Design

When Ajaz Ahmed first came across the internet in the mid-1990s, it set his imagination alight. Immediately anticipating the scope and power of this new medium, he founded a creative digital agency that today leads the world in innovation and quality of service. Yet despite his accomplishments Ahmed is still as wowed by advancing technology as he ever was.

Unbounded enthusiasm

Interviewing Ajaz Ahmed is a confusing experience. AKQA's co-founder and chairman enjoys chatting to journalists. Just not about the history of his business. He'll discuss with relish the rise of internet applications, the meritocratic nature of doing business online and the importance of web-based learning. But when it comes to the facts of his own company he's elusive.

Even the meaning of the name AKQA is a closely guarded secret, and like in the case of Adidas before it, has been the subject of speculation. In the eighties kids who bought their trainers thought Adidas stood for 'all day I dream about sport'. Today some in the media speculate that AKQA means 'all known questions answered' – it doesn't. No one exactly knows what it stands for.

They like a bit of mystery over at AKQA. But as the world's leading independent online brand consultancy, with 800 employees in five locations and $150m turnover, the company has every right to have some fun. It has a trophy cabinet that would impress Man United (in the first quarter of 2009 alone it hoovered up five industry awards – the first agency to achieve that) and has been the envy of its peers since it was founded by a group of friends 15 years ago.

New media, new needs

When we meet at the upmarket Wolseley café in London's Mayfair, Ahmed looks like he's just hopped off a skateboard. Dressed all in black with an open shirt and trainers he appears considerably younger than his 36 years. Try to pick the chairman out of a line up and you'd get it wrong every time. I suspect that's exactly the look he's after.

Ahmed was convinced to start up AKQA in 1995 after being "shown the web" by a friend at Bath University. "I was at my next-door neighbour's house. He flicked on his computer and showed me a picture and when I said 'big deal', he told me it had come from America. He was showing me the embryonic web and I was stunned. A light went on and I knew that all brands would want to communicate using this medium somehow.

"As it transpired, a lot of brands knew the internet was coming and recognised that online marketing and 'e-commerce' would be important, but they didn't understand what it meant; so there was a slight climate of fear – they could see patterns would change in the future and had to respond."

In the short space of time from that day to this, brands fell over themselves to get online and develop a web presence that would immerse the user, help them 'interact' and show consumers a good time, all whilst hammering home their message. New digital brands and technological advances forced the breakneck evolution of consumer laptops and mobile phones, and now goods could be bought anytime, anywhere, on just about anything that goes 'beep'.

It was in this volatile, fast-changing environment that AKQA grew to pre-eminence as digital advisor to the big brands, who mostly knew what they wanted from the internet but had no idea how to achieve it. An early example of how the business stamped its authority on the market was its work with BMW.

No template, no repetition

"It's really difficult to believe this now, but before BMW all car websites were nothing to do with cars," he grins. "Car manufacturers would have lifestyle publications as their websites. So we saw our role as making this site interactive and service-orientated."

For BMW, AKQA created the first approved online used-car directory, allowing customers to configure and buy their vehicle of choice. It sounds like an obvious idea today, but at the time it was unusual and badly received by the trade press, who were critical of this disruptive new direction.

And then *Top Gear* came along. "They reviewed all the car websites and said BMW's was the best. They listed all the reasons on air, and overnight the project was transformed into a success," Ahmed remembers. Then followed rave reviews in the *Financial Times* and other mainstream newspapers and AKQA's reputation was sealed.

Today, not all AKQA projects are so practical or groundbreaking; many are straightforward branding exercises. But the key to the business' accomplishments is that every new client is viewed in a fresh light and with a focus on its specific individual needs – there is no template and no repetition.

That approach earns AKQA unparalleled loyalty in its market with brands such as Virgin, Nike and McDonald's coming back year after year, for more than a decade in some cases. Honesty is also a big deal for Ahmed; the business earns kudos for turning away jobs that aren't central to its remit and for admitting when its order books are full.

"Many businesses make the mistake of taking on too many clients when they can't service projects. We've had clients that we've worked with for more than a decade and that is unheard of in our industry. 99% of the time they had more respect for us because we were so honest with them. The last thing they wanted was for us to take something on that we couldn't deliver."

When all about you are losing their heads

This methodical and grounded approach was one of the reasons AKQA flourished after the dotcom bust when other online brands faltered or disappeared altogether. While some businesses overstretched themselves, Ahmed stuck to time-honoured principles and set a path for sustainable growth.

"There had been similar bubbles in older technology markets; think of the hardware and software companies that were legendary in the 80s and 90s but don't exist now. For me, the dotcom bubble reflected that, so we wouldn't work with them if they didn't have a solid business model. We focused on the blue-chips.

"We never had the crazy growth period through the dotcom boom but when it flipped we grew. It seems like genius now, but it was very straightforward: you take the long-term view and you remember your duty of care. We didn't want to hire people who would lose their jobs in the future.

"We turned away contracts worth millions and nobody understood it, but afterwards everyone did." In the aftermath of the dotcom crash, says Ahmed, "we were one of the only firms in our market that was a proven brand with a proven track record. We had a good reputation and a great team, our trajectory was not explosive." It was the key to success. Now as then, "it's a solid business and grows sustainably".

Focus, not 'full-service'

Similarly, Ahmed has resisted the urge to diversify his services into offline marketing and media production. Though there are many 'full-service' media businesses that manage to wear several hats at once, Ahmed thinks that taking the business into new directions would detract from what it does well. His favourite term is 'less is more'.

"When we started the agency we never set out be the biggest, we wanted to create influential work," Ahmed claims. "But that ethic has turned us into one of the largest independent agencies in the world right now. It's the by-product of focus on quality rather than size."

SYED AHMED

Hot Air?

Pilloried in the media and written off by the public as a boastful chancer, Syed Ahmed is out to prove to the world that he has earned the title 'entrepreneur'.

Kicking the 'clown'

Since he appeared on the second series of *The Apprentice* early in 2006, Syed Ahmed has been lampooned in the press and portrayed as a clown. The show's contestants are all kicked about by gloating journalists, but somehow Ahmed attracted more punishment than anyone else before or since.

Was his performance that diabolical? He was arrogant, certainly, but 90% of the cast fit that criteria; including the ever-popular Lord Sugar himself. Ahmed survived four turns in the boardroom before being fired in episode ten because he was too "high risk" for the boss. A very respectable innings.

He wasn't especially nasty, either, in spite of all those boardroom encounters, which in subsequent series have become opportunities for contestants to stab each other viciously in the front, not just in the back. To his credit, he didn't raise his voice during these bouts and at least tried to build a constructive argument against his opponents.

No. Journalists, like the rest of us, enjoy beating Ahmed up because of his unswerving self-belief, which borders on – then falls helplessly into – fantasy. Upon speaking to Ahmed you are led to believe that he has no weaknesses, that he is in fact steel-plated with the mind of a master entrepreneur.

He tells you he's made mistakes and that he's on a learning curve, but he doesn't want you to believe it. His language is hyperbolic, sprinkled with references to "teams of engineers", "breaking the mould" and "the most...in the world". He also uses hackneyed business speak without irony.

And unlike most entrepreneurs, he won't acknowledge that being in business is sometimes not glamorous; that when you start you might not have staff or turnover or even a reputation – and that you might not succeed. His involvement in his first business, an IT recruitment consultancy, was fairly short-lived, and the website doesn't exactly scream "success", but the way Ahmed describes it you'd think he founded Adecco.

His self-possession, poise and augmented speak are symptoms of what makes Ahmed entrepreneurial: an absolute refusal to accept when he is beaten. Even as Lord Sugar levelled his finger at him, Ahmed was angling for an escape. In a real sense this should be applauded, but for the press it represents an excellent excuse to seize upon all of his failings.

"You have to deal with the crap"

Unfortunately for Ahmed he has more than a few. Some are cause for concern like his conviction in 2006 for drink-driving for which he received a two-month suspended jail sentence and a three-year driving ban. Some are clown-like, such as his brief appearance on Sky television's *Cirque de Celebrité* or his failure to qualify for a celebrity football team, again filmed for Sky.

Some have been downright sad, like the media's treatment of his and fellow *Apprentice* contestant Michelle Dewberry's relationship which developed during the show and continued for a short-time after. The couple were door-stepped by paparazzi and received widespread coverage when Dewberry became pregnant, only to lose the baby in a miscarriage after just a few months.

"PR can be damaging," says Ahmed as we chat over coffee in the bowels of London's Adam Street club. "If you want to go there and court journalists then you're in for a surprise because there is no control. Occasionally you have to deal with the crap.

"It was difficult after the show because you lose all privacy. I was a journalist's dream coming off the back of *The Apprentice*, having a relationship with Michelle and the misfortune that came after that – it was a very sensitive and difficult time."

After his driving ban Ahmed was again embroiled in controversy when his former business partner at IT People, Aftab Ahmed, was accused of defrauding Portsmouth Football Club director Terry Brady in a loan deal that went wrong. Although cleared of all wrongdoing and volunteering evidence to the police, Syed Ahmed was again dragged through the media spotlight by his hair.

But he faced down his demons with customary doggedness. Since the tumultuous days of 2006 he has founded SA Vortex, a hand-drying technology business, Get Launched, a website-creation business, and even established a charity with the aim of helping poverty-stricken people in Bangladesh. He has also amassed a team of high-profile entrepreneurs to help his business pursuits and again used TV to create interest in his products.

Dry before you buy

Like some of the best businesses, SA Vortex started on a whim. "I use the gym quite a lot so I thought there was a gap for a more cost-effective and hygienic way of drying after the shower," Ahmed asserts. But it wasn't until a TV production company approached him with a proposal to follow his attempt to launch a business that Ahmed put his idea into practice.

For Sky it was no doubt another opportunity to film him flapping around and making himself look silly, an opportunity that he partly delivered on, but for Ahmed it represented a real chance to exploit a niche and revolutionise an industry. When the cameras stopped rolling, Ahmed made real progress. In the three years since the idea for drying machines was first conceived, SA Vortex has shifted its focus from an all-over dryer to a simple contraption that dries hands fast and saves energy.

Describing its latest incarnation, he is typically colourful: "We created a drying system that heats air without using heating elements. It uses compression like in a bicycle pump to heat air to 60 degrees. It's a mini-jet engine that fits in your palm, compresses the air and squeezes it out through a vortex."

I suggest to Ahmed that this greener, more efficient technology would place SA Vortex in direct competition with renowned entrepreneurs like Sir James Dyson, whose super-fast Airblade system has made a mockery of other hand dryers by winning a host of awards and turning the market on its head.

But Ahmed is now growing in confidence: "We have saved energy on World Dryer, the market leader, by 80%. Yet when we built a box and put the engine in it we were drying hands in seconds."

Turning to his soon-to-be arch-rival, he adds: "We use 70% less energy than the Dyson hand dryer. We're smaller, greener and cleaner – and just as fast. Ours is a completely new design and we're looking forward to surprising the market."

The new SA Vortex website is equally boastful: "The Vortex hand dryer, the greenest, fastest and quietest hand dryer in its class." For good measure, it adds: "When compared to competitors' dryers it's easy to realise cost savings of £300k to £1m over the life of the dryer." It even boasts a 97% saving versus an equivalent use of paper towels.

There is nothing to suggest that any of this has been substantiated, particularly not the claim that the Vortex has a lifespan ten times longer than competitors using 'brushed motor technology', whatever that is. But Ahmed has created something that certainly looks the part and he has attracted two rounds of funding for the device.

Not just this, but successful entrepreneurs are getting in on the project, including Thomas Power, founder of Ecademy, who joined Angels Den creator Bill Borrow and Tesco.com founder Martin Cunningson.

Meanwhile Ahmed assures me that at least one potential buyer has offered "a large sum of money" for the technology.

Of course, until SA Vortex starts selling units in the thousands the media will continue to treat Syed Ahmed as a mock entrepreneur, and there's a good chance that the derision will continue even after *The Apprentice* wannabe has proved himself a success. But that's what you get for daring to tell the world you're about to succeed.

The irony is that having become labelled a flop, I worry that this entrepreneur will struggle to fill column inches if he achieves his business dreams. But maybe we want out anti-heroes to remain just that.

SARAH BEENY

From Home Improver to Dotcom Millionaire

Famous for advising predominantly newbie property entrepreneurs, Sarah Beeny has carved out a secondary career as an internet entrepreneur. She is arguably more successful in the latter role despite her public image of a hammer-wielding wonder woman – that and her self-confessed tech ineptness.

A real entrepreneur

It would be easy to dismiss Sarah Beeny as a famous person cashing in on her celebrity. Television doesn't pay that well on its own so most presenters set up sidelines with books, adverts and merchandise. But in Beeny's case it runs a lot deeper. She had her sleeves rolled up long before appearing on TV and to this day rates her presenting career as a sideshow to her business interests.

She should not be confused with other female celebrity 'entrepreneurs'; pop stars and actresses mainly, who lend their name to perfume, lingerie and jewellery lines and trust their brand to professional executives. Beeny founds her businesses in the truest sense of the word. She comes up with the idea, sources the help she'll need to get it off the ground and plays an active part in running and promoting the business.

War on the drinks-fridge brigade

So far Beeny has always co-founded her companies with at least one other person (her husband Graham Swift is also a trusted business partner), buying them into the project with the carrot of a big equity slice, before stepping back from the day-to-day running once the project is alive and kicking.

When I speak to Beeny she is in the process of launching Tepilo.com, a house-trading website named after a made-up castle which featured in bedtime stories told by her father when she was little. "It sounded like a magical place," she says wistfully. "I named the site after it because everyone wants to live in their dream home."

The business case is much more down-to-earth. Beeny wants to save you money when you move home and in the process curb the market for rogue estate agents who she feels no longer represent value for money.

"There are some really bad estate agents as well as some good ones, but basically there are far too many of them. The majority are inexperienced, but they can still be really expensive with fees around 2-3% of your house's sale value," she laments.

"Do their fancy window displays or drinks fridges or branded cars help them serve you? No, not really. But your fees pay for them. I don't want to get rid of estate agents, they have a place for big or unusual sales, but for an average two-bed flat in a city somewhere they're just not needed."

Tepilo.com is not the first of its kind, but its predecessors have by-and-large floundered in an industry where trust is all-important and homebuyers are reassured by the perceived safety net of middlemen. Putting her own face to the project (literally, there's a huge picture of Beeny on the homepage) should allay fears and encourage the sort of numbers needed to populate such an ambitious website.

It is early days – the site having gone live just a few months before our interview – and a search for all properties in London (population circa 8m) brings up a grand total of 72 for sale. Sellers also have to upload and maintain a profile, and take care of showing people around their property as well as all negotiations – hurdles, perhaps, to the sensitive and time-strapped (though Beeny provides a series of comprehensive guides to help). But Beeny has been here before and knows that patience is a virtue when it comes to building a user base.

Painstaking patience

It was the same with her other online project, dating website mysinglefriend.com, founded in 2005. Today a London-wide search for men and women across all the various dating preferences throws up something like 25,000 results, but it took several months to tempt the first 100 people online.

"I had an image of it taking off really quickly but it was painstaking at the start, which is why I'm a lot more relaxed about Tepilo" she admits. "It was like pulling teeth. I was on the phone offering to pay people to upload their friend and it wasn't until we reached about 300 that it started to roll."

People signing up to mysinglefriend could do so for free for two years while the founders developed interest in the website. Today singles have a few pricing options including a basic no-charge membership. The frills package costs £18 a month, stretching to £50 for six months if you don't fancy your chances of pulling quickly.

Tepilo is also free to join. But unlike its dating website cousin, Beeny wants to keep it free forever, potentially making money through sponsorship and affiliate deals starting at an unspecified later date. To be honest, she's not completely sure what will happen.

Her attitude contrasts with nuts-and-bolts entrepreneurs who structure their business future in one-, three- and five-year plans. She has no marketing strategy, no revenue targets and no solid projections. But that suits her just fine. Being independently wealthy, she is in the fortunate position of not needing all her ventures to be overnight successes.

"It doesn't have millions of pounds invested or a big TV campaign planned. I guess our strategy is viral marketing: we make a great product, tell people about it and hopefully they will tell others. We want quality over quantity to begin with, so we're allowing it to build slowly. Hopefully the quantity will come in time."

Thick skin

Although Tepilo is in its infancy, the latent threat it poses is stirring up a backlash from senior agents against the *Property Ladder* presenter: "Some people have been incredibly defensive, but as yet they haven't been able to construct a sensible argument against buying and selling houses in this way.

"One comment that springs to mind was from someone very high up in the industry, who said 'I hope it doesn't work'. I think it says something if that's the best they can come up with," she says with a grin. "This isn't a slanging match, so I'll keep on ignoring it and focus on making the business work."

Beeny's thick skin comes from years in male dominated environments. Proving unacademic at school she attempted to forge a career as an actress, before failing to get into drama school. A stint travelling the world and subsequently a string of odd jobs led to her founding a property-development business.

Partnered with her husband and advised by her architect father she went from project to project before a chance meeting at a hen party led to a successful screen test and the creation of *Property Ladder* and a host of spin-off productions.

"We were around building sites all the time when I was young so I feel I know buildings really well. I love things to do with the home and ultimately my whole career centres around relationships and comfortable living," she smiles.

"The entrepreneur bit comes from my father. He was obsessed by Richard Branson and Anita Roddick, so whenever I came home from school with a bad grade he'd go and find a newspaper cut-out from somewhere and show me what they had achieved."

Beeny is a homely entrepreneur who won't be distracted from her twin loves of family and the home. She has a simple approach and doesn't aggressively chase profit, despite what she might advise on the telly. And while her job is also her hobby, 80-hour weeks are not her style. Many entrepreneurs I know could use a leaf from her book.

LORD KARAN BILIMORIA CBE DL

The Beer Peer Who Wants World Domination

Karan Bilimoria started out in business with nothing but £20,000 of university debt. Twenty years and successive twists and turns later he partnered Cobra Beer with one of the biggest brewers in the world and now is poised to fulfil his dream of creating a global drinks brand.

A touchable sense of upheaval

Ever since he founded Cobra Beer in 1989, Lord Bilimoria never sat comfortably atop his business empire. From the mid-90s sales growth was effortless with double-digit increases annually, yet, for the first 20 years at least, Cobra never turned a profit and flirted with disaster on many occasions.

This is one of those occasions. As I sit opposite Bilimoria in Cobra's old Fulham headquarters there is a touchable sense of upheaval around us. One month earlier he saved the business from collapse with a pre-pack administration deal and investment from international brewing heavyweight Molson Coors.

Molson paid £14m for a 50.1% stake in the business, but stipulated that Cobra would need to shed its debt for the deal to go through. Hence the pre-pack, which effectively meant Cobra could shake off its creditors before entering into the tie up.

Bilimoria is keen to play down the hurt this caused investors and suppliers and he insists that the level of unpaid debt is "a tiny fraction" of the £70-£75m reported in the press, but his tired face and hushed tones betray his regret regarding the less-savoury aspects of the arrangement.

Cobra's problems stemmed from Bilimoria's choices in financing its growth, which, incidentally, also played a large part in its success. The company fell tens of millions of pounds into the red despite consistent growth and eventually it lost the lines of credit that powered its expansion.

Bilimoria's strategy was to focus on high-growth and to sacrifice net profits while developing the business, his rationale being that the business would become instantly profitable in the hands of an acquiring company if it was able to absorb Cobra's costs.

Hazy but not lazy

Bilimoria started his business while working part-time to pay bills. He worked with his business partner Arjun Reddy – who exited in 1995 – during the evening and at weekends. "I conducted seven months of market research before even starting the production, making sure I had the concept right and that I would be able to sell the product," he recollects, in a clipped, educated accent that is more Cambridge than Bangalore.

After going to India to develop the beer, they imported their first containers to Britain. The pair delivered one consignment to a customer in Newcastle and one to a London wholesaler. But the embryonic Cobra product failed a quality test at the London firm because it was "too hazy", forcing the entrepreneurs to offload the stock by selling to restaurants, bars and pubs door-to-door.

This, claims Bilimoria, gave them the model for sales that endures to this day. The restaurateurs, in particular, appreciated the smoother, less gassy formula which underpins the brand. Today it is stocked in 6,000 restaurants in the UK.

"It's about being adaptable and flexible"

"It's about being adaptable and flexible," he stresses. "Here you are, having never sold a bottle of beer in your life, with one of the largest wholesalers in the country letting you down. What do you do? We were stuck with half a container, so we got out there and sold."

It was the first of a number of hurdles for the business. In 1996, having experienced a doubling of demand, Bilimoria was forced to uproot production from Bangalore, the spiritual home of Cobra, and bring it to Bedford, to a plant which could cope with the required level of manufacture.

Friends advised Bilimoria that removing the brand from its heartland would spell disaster, but a spot of market research revealed that customers were much more concerned about the flavour and the experience of the beer than the authenticity of its background.

In 1997, the problem repeated itself when, having expanded its production base to Belgium and a main plant in Poland, the Polish manufacturers were taken over by South African brewers SAB Miller. Despite a contract in place to supply Cobra, SAB "made it abundantly clear" that they didn't want to.

"We'd started looking for another Eastern European supplier, but the answer was right under our noses and we moved production back to the UK, to three separate breweries with state-of-the-art Swedish, German and Swiss technology, using Irish investment and a British workforce in northwest England.

"It is the most fantastic, space-age plant and we actually saved money manufacturing over here. People say UK manufacturing's dead; far from it. We turned a huge disadvantage, again something that could have really harmed our business in a big way, into an advantage by being flexible and adaptable."

Boycott nightmare

But the most hard-to-get-over bump in the road, before the administration, came in 1998 when a magazine jointly owned by

Bilimoria and a friend published an article on service in Indian restaurants. The critique angered the restaurant community that was Cobra's lifeblood and resulted in a boycott of the beer. Bilimoria himself had never seen the article, let alone given it the green light.

At the same time Cobra was undergoing its first big advertising drive. Created by Saatchi, the multi-media campaign spanned Tube and bus ads, newspapers and radio. Anticipating a big increase in demand, Bilimoria ordered new regional depots to be found or built.

But the boycott, which lasted a whole year, crushed the business. The freshly-opened depots shut almost immediately, while the workforce of 120 people shrunk to just 20. The business model changed to target flat growth and the business' bank began advising it to wind up operations.

"It was a nightmare," shudders Bilimoria. "Through that period, if we had not been adaptable and flexible, we would have been finished, absolutely finished. Because of the integrity and the strength of the brand, eventually the restaurateurs lifted the boycott, but if we hadn't been able to do that, we would not have survived."

Karan Bilimoria is a sturdy man with a bold, lined face that helps him to convey an easy air of authority. Patient and softly spoken, he is the very image of a British peer. His father was a lieutenant-general in the Indian army, and Bilimoria learned to lead at an early age; a talent which, combined with his professional qualifications, gave him the ideal grounding for success in business.

As an army commander, General Bilimoria was in of charge 350,000 soldiers and his son was able to absorb lessons in delegation, creating efficiencies and building morale. He also learned to go the extra mile and do not just what he was told, but a little bit more, so as to impress.

"We're proud of our base and we always want to be the best beer to drink with Indian food," he enthuses. "But we also want people to drink Cobra because they love the beer in its own right."

BRAD BURTON

The Redeemer of Business Networking

After a tumultuous career, including one failed business and two stints on the dole, Brad Burton co-founded 4Networking, a set of breakfast network groups for entrepreneurs that dares to break the mould in something that had threatened to become stale and unproductive: the networking event. He explains how self-motivation proved the difference between a thriving business and jobseekers' allowance.

No excuses

When I meet Brad Burton he's fresh from a big argument which took place on 4Networking's online forum. Burton, who starts a good number of the threads himself, suggested that 2009's economic slump was not as bad as everyone thought it would be.

"Not really much of a recession was it?" he postulates to the forum's 22,000 members – most of whom are business owners and entrepreneurs. The near 200 responses fly in thick and fast, and range from tepid endorsements to angry rebukes.

Not for the first time, Burton finds himself in hot water with his own people because of his consummate lack of subtlety. But this brassy, uncompromising businessman lives and dies by his trademark candour, and it has won him more friends and followers than enemies.

"I've had several personal recessions in my life and it might have been tough but I have never starved to death yet. It's all too easy for people to use the recession as an excuse as to why they're failing, when actually the reason a lot of businesses fail is because of poor business practices."

Burton comes into contact with a broad spectrum of British businesses in his stewardship of 4Networking (or 4N to its friends), a joined-up network comprising 200 local business clusters that organise regular breakfast networking events as well as parties and other social engagements.

He cites examples of one business he knows charging £37 to print out a PDF and another that treated a £25,000 contract the same as a £1000 one. Both went under in the recession, but Burton says the entrepreneurs involved will learn from their mistakes and come back stronger.

50% business, 50% fun

Thankfully his own business is a different story to the contemporary mismanagement he laments. Formed in 2006, its wobbles took place before the recession and in the last few years it has benefited from the increased demand for free mentoring and support among Britain's struggling entrepreneurs. The network develops new locations on a weekly basis and is poised to expand overseas.

He believes the organisation's growing popularity is down to its informal approach, which is officially comprised of 50% business, 50% fun; that and the lack of any worthwhile opposition.

"You get some so-called 'open networking' events which are like a school disco. People standing around the walls eating *vol-au-vents* and looking out for their mates. Then there are organisations that regiment everything you do and don't allow communication between their groups. They take your money and then slap a load of limitations on you. It's stacked in favour of the house and the dealer always wins. You have to get invited by members, speak when you're spoken to, and basically it's a load of bollocks," he says in his customary rapid-fire delivery.

From chaos to dance off

Burton, who in his early career developed a talent for marketing, gleefully set about the task of constructing a bargain-bucket promotional drive that he hoped would attract 4N's first members.

"It was guerrilla marketing at its finest," he laughs. "That is my thing and I enjoy it. I parked up outside a networking event just as people were leaving and handed out letters explaining why they shouldn't sign up to it and why they should come to us.

"The first meeting, though, was chaos. The pair had to ask for money up front (they had forgotten to mention payment beforehand), there were far too many attendees for everyone to have their allotted one-minute introduction and when one-to-one sessions began, confusion reigned.

"Tim just said to me, 'This is rubbish; we've got to do something'.

"So we just said, 'Right, stand up and talk to the people you want to talk to'. Voooom! That was when the penny dropped. The format we use now is not much different and it only took three meetings to get the structure for each event spot on."

Two of the assembled 72 signed up for £250 annual memberships on the spot, and Brad and Tim spent the money on more marketing material – starting with business cards. The next meeting took place two weeks later and 18 people returned. Within 12 months 4N had established 12 independent groups in South-West England.

The flexible model caught on and new groups cropped up with increasing regularity, spreading the brand north and east, eventually encircling London in a Schlieffen-like pincer movement, before at last pushing inside the M25.

Burton kept up his guerrilla marketing too, recently organising a no-holds-barred 'dance off' with fellow 4Ner Eddie Johnson, co-founder of graphic design business Kimeera. The event was filmed and released as a viral video. To the delight of members it was picked up by a handful of business news websites and spread around the internet.

Can you ride a moped?

But not everything has been plain sailing for 4N. On two occasions it has parted ways with its web developers and lost money as a result. The first developer pulled out unexpectedly just as the website was attracting serious interest from members and non-members alike.

4N nearly came unstuck a second time when Burton decreed that the group was big enough to draw in new members from word-of-mouth only. Group chiefs no longer canvassed for new members and sign-ups gradually trickled to a stop.

Burton nevertheless continued to spend on merchandise and marketing materials until the money nearly ran out. In mid-2008, with the business established and growing healthily, it nearly went belly up because of a cash-flow issue: "It was close to falling over just based on my whim," he remembers.

Burton's 'personal recessions' before founding 4N were also instructive experiences. In his late thirties and a successful businessman he has spent four years in the past claiming unemployment benefits and when his first venture, a marketing consultancy, failed to fire, he resorted to delivering pizzas to make ends meet.

"I was watching Jeremy Kyle one day instead of working – there's no point pretending to work when you're your own boss. The phone rang and it was the wife, and I thought 'shit' she's in full-time employment, the baby is in childcare at £6.50 an hour, and I'm watching Jeremy Kyle.

"She said 'How's it going?' and I said, 'Okay, irons in the fire'. She said, 'When the bank starts taking irons in the fire for mortgage payments you let me know'. I went and got the pizza delivery job that day. They asked 'Can you ride a moped?' I said yeah. 'You've got the job'."

Now, whenever he's called up for speaking engagements, Burton takes a pizza box with him. "I used to be dead embarrassed about it," he chuckles, "but now I'm proud to have taken the step; I should have done it eight months earlier. It was a cathartic experience. I thought now that I have hit rock bottom, how do I get out of this?"

And get out of it he has.

JAMES CAAN

From Lahore to the Den Via a Recruitment Empire

James Caan is the thinking man's Dragon. Meditative, impassive and often the last to decide on an investment opportunity, he doesn't fit the fire-breathing stereotype of the BBC show. But with an investment portfolio of 40 businesses, Caan's lack of on-screen bravado belies his ferocious appetite for enterprise.

"That's why I work weekends"

You and I know him as the laid-back one from *Dragons' Den*, but television is far from a priority for James Caan. He works seven days a week on the upkeep of his private equity empire, which guards the interests of a combined turnover of £400m.

Hamilton Bradshaw, Caan's private equity company, is an impressive outfit. It is headquartered in an immaculate Mayfair office on a row of Victorian six-storey stucco-fronted properties. You know you're at the right address because the marble approach has an 'HB' seal. The waiting room offers a selection of investment titles for your perusal and mounted on the wall is a plasma TV proudly displaying Caan's timeline of achievements.

Caan, who changed his name from Nazim Khan to that of a famous American actor because it "seemed like a good idea at the time", bought the cavernous former townhouse for £4.2m at the beginning of 2009 as the property market bottomed out. By the time I pass through the front door a matter of months later it has already nearly doubled in value.

I am led upstairs to a wonderfully spacious office. Despite a change of purpose the room retains its original character, with opulent furnishings more accustomed to the home than the workplace.

Dotted about is evidence of his celebrity status and business achievements. A beaming Caan is pictured with political figures and celebrities as well as his fellow Dragons, while trophies, plaques and certificates denoting various triumphs are liberally dotted about.

As I enter the room he is at the opposite end discussing stocks and shares with one of his many analysts. "There must be some reason why it's gone up 10% this morning, take a look at it will you?" he says before turning to greet me. After further discussion his colleague exits and Caan parks himself at one end of a large glass desk that just whispers, 'he's the boss'.

He breaks into some nicotine gum, then scoops up a stress ball in the shape of a brain. Teasing it between his hands, he begins to talk, giving a few questions the respect of a full answer, dismissing others with a casual yes or no.

"Of all the Dragons, I live closest to TV, so I might start the day talking to BBC Breakfast," explains Caan, illuminating me as to how he divides his day. "On the way I might stop off at one of my portfolio businesses; afterwards I'll meet with my investment team. In the afternoon I'll meet my investment director for our real-estate business. I might talk to the bank, pay a visit to my forex guy and my equities analyst before close of play."

But it doesn't stop there. Caan reckons he keeps five dinner engagements a week on average, mostly with business contacts. This from a man who, having already built up and sold one global business, has an estimated £60m to his name. I think an explanation is needed.

"I'm always motivated and excited about my job. It has to be one of the best in the world. What drives me is intellectual stimulation and the opportunity of doing different things. It's my hobby and my passion and I love it. That's why I work weekends."

Harvard and Lahore

It was ever thus. Caan worked for 14 years straight developing his middle-management recruitment business, Alexander Mann, and when he resigned as CEO in 1999, selling a chunk of the business as he did so, his 'time out' period included a Harvard MBA and an audacious philanthropic school project in Lahore.

"Being 40 and quite successful I'd meet people and they would ask me what I studied and I had to tell them I didn't. Harvard was an amazing experience and afterwards I basically faffed around, buying things – a yacht, a house in France – and doing things on a whim.

"One day I was having lunch with someone and we talked about Pakistan; they asked me when I had last been to Lahore, and I was shocked when I realised it had been 30 years. So the next day I booked flights," he says with a smile and a shrug.

A few days later, having sampled first-hand the lack of academic opportunity in the city of his birth, Caan resolved to build a school with his own money and without state subsidy. Shrugging off warnings surrounding his lack of experience, he went to work with designers, planners and local educators.

The resultant Abdul Rashid Khan Campus, with its library, modern IT lab and science faculty was instantly oversubscribed and today educates 500 kids. Caan named it after his father, also an entrepreneur, who came to the UK unable to read or write when the then-'Khan' junior was just ten years old. As we speak, plans are in motion for a new secondary school, too.

From nothing to £400m turnover

Alexander Mann, the proceeds of the sale of which made all this possible, started like most businesses: with a good idea. In 1985, a 25-year-old Caan noticed a gap in the recruitment market for an executive search business targeting middle managers.

"I thought that middle-managers were just as important to organisations as its top brass, maybe more so. Why not headhunt them too? At the time, if you wanted a regional manager you had to go through press adverts. I was convinced that wasn't the best method.

"Today I think the slice of the market I created is worth about £5bn in fee income. It's one of the largest areas of service delivery. The business was successful because of the strategy I put in place and the people I hired. But you have to have a good idea in the first place; that was mine."

Caan took the business from nothing to £130m turnover by 1999, and by the time he sold his last chunk of equity in 2008, that figure had yawned to £400m. It took Caan seven years to set up shop outside the UK, but by the time seven more passed it was trading in 30 countries across the globe.

The bumps in the road

Quick growth and healthy figures are not the whole story, Caan assures me. He has never been lucky enough to succeed without at least a few bumps in the road: "It wasn't plain sailing by any means. I'm a strong believer that if anything could go wrong in business then it probably will.

"A successful entrepreneur is not someone that avoids problems but someone who is prepared to handle them when they crop up. That's especially true of growing a business internationally, where you have to deal with different sets of governance, compliance, tax, legal and cultural rules."

The economic downturn had a mixed impact on his business interests. Some are fighting fit, but others – predominantly the customer-focused ones – are a little green around the gills. One firm, a recruitment business serving the construction industry, has collapsed completely. But HB itself has never been busier.

"It's a very exciting time in the cycle. There is a supply of investment opportunities but very little demand for them so prices have fallen dramatically. We exited most of our commitments at the height of the boom in 2007, so now we're spending quite aggressively," he grins.

"We think we are investing at the bottom of the cycle and as long you don't believe that the world is ending, then prices have to recover. Will they return to the dizzying heights? Who knows? But they have to come back from where they were in 2009."

GERRY CALABRESE

Serving up Cocktails at a Canter

Gerry Calabrese founded the Hoxton Pony just as Shoreditch's coolest kids were upping sticks and finding new spiritual homes to the north and east of London's financial district. Left over were the slightly less cool but considerably wealthier me-toos, which suits him down to the ground.

Ahead of the trends

The Hoxton Pony sits at the centre of Shoreditch nightlife. Located halfway up Curtain Road and surrounded by similarly trendy, or trendier, venues (The Queen of Hoxton, Dream Bags Jaguar Shoes, The Macbeth, and Beach Blanket Babylon), it has self-consciously aped the area's aura of alternative chic.

"We're like the Marmite of Shoreditch," says Calabrese with a smirk, as he escorts me to the venue's office in the basement; "you either love us or you hate us." And while the venue has 2000 regulars on its guest list, a newsletter following of 40,000 and took £6.5m in its first year, there are a number of detractors who want to conserve the town's bohemian roots.

"It's a balancing act in this area. The Pony is quite polished for Shoreditch and I think if you start allowing suits in after nine o'clock it's not the right look. We try to keep the music quite edgy and keep the crowd quite edgy as well. That way you counterbalance the gleam of the place.

"Otherwise it's quite a negative marketing exercise, because this place is almost the commercial face of Shoreditch. People travel here from West London and they'll want to come here as the other places are a bit too risqué or they're not comfortable or they haven't got nice drinks on offer, but they still want to be perceived as cool."

As a slick bar in an arty boho postcode, Calabrese has to keep on top of the Hoxton Pony's vibe, and he reviews his marketing plan on a quarterly basis. Because it's Hoxton, his observation of the trends that come and go can lead to some peculiar judgments.

"The people who are coming to be perceived as cool may not like the music we play, but if we played the music they like they wouldn't come here any more. So it's quite complicated. Trends and music tastes change quickly here, so we have to stay ahead of that."

The art of a good night

Calabrese is schooled in the art of a good night. He has worked in or with some prime London attractions including Lab, Dust and Sex in the City. He set up his own promotions company and became immersed in late-night culture, and from 2004 he ran Farringdon haunt Meet, a three-tier 24-hour cocktail bar which made his name as a mixologist.

Eager to leave school and start earning money, he got his first break as a teenager working in the restaurant of the Lanesborough Hotel in London, having received a leg up from his father, world-famous and multi-award-winning bartender Salvatore 'The Maestro' Calabrese.

After a stint at The Ivy and having grown tired of the restaurant business, Salvatore was again Gerry's inspiration as he worked his way up the late-night ladder as a barman, bar manager and latterly bar owner.

"My dad is my idol," he admits. "If I can achieve one-tenth of what my old man has in his life I will be one very happy guy. As a bartender you strive to immortalise yourself with one great drink and my old man's done a couple.

I've carved out a different place for myself – what I do is mainly music led and late-night ventures, so it works."

"It's all about relationships"

On top of taking advantage of the good Calabrese name, Calabrese junior expertly employed the 'not what you know, but who you know' school of business. Having rubbed shoulders in countless bars, restaurants and events full of fashionistas, he knew exactly who to turn to when creating the Hoxton Pony, from the architect who designed the layout to the accountant who does the books.

Some of the staff working at the Hoxton Pony today were with him when he started as a barkeep nine years ago. But it doesn't stop there. Using proceeds from the sale of Meet, the bar he ran single-handedly immediately prior to the Pony, Calabrese has collaborated with two pals on sideline businesses: a doorman security firm and, closer to his heart, a new brand of gin.

"I'm very impatient and always want to do stuff," he enthuses and he shuffles in his seat. "It's called Calabrese Pearson Gin or CP Gin. We did everything: found the recipe, found the producer and worked with them in the lab to get the recipe exactly right.

"Why gin? I love it; gin's my favourite spirit; we're a gin bar here and we have 34 types of gin and for me, this is a gin aimed at young people, because most people drink vodka from the age of 16 to 24. I wanted to develop something that's a viable alternative to the straightforward vodka and mixer."

This is clearly more than a pet project for Calabrese, who reels off with vigour the details of ingredients, process and the market. He has a ten-year plan for product development and has released it to the on-trade first, plus a few selected retailers, in order to develop an air of exclusivity in the brand.

The cocktail production line

Calabrese says his hands-on approach in managing the Hoxton Pony is due to regular disappointments in the past. When he arrived at Meet he discovered there was no stock room and instead of rows of bottles behind the bar (as you would expect) there was a giant antique mirror. Not exactly practical.

Erasing the memory of this, he describes his standard of one-step bartending, which means each server has their own cash till, drink-making tools and fridges filled with ingredients a single step away. He spent £75,000 on the back bar alone and is confident of a return on that investment.

"In a 400-capacity venue, normally you'll have around 12 people serving. I have six. The reason for that is I try very hard to employ the right people. I've got a very low staff turnover and I've probably had one person leave voluntarily since we started. That, coupled with the system that we've got in place, makes it work."

And work it does. Despite cancelled bookings in the run-up to Christmas 2008, the Hoxton Pony took up to £35,000 on Friday nights that December. The warm early summer months in 2009 also had a detrimental impact (it has no outside space to speak of) but the inevitable rain that followed balanced the books.

Calabrese now has his sights set on developing management contracts for big events away from Shoreditch and making his new gin a roaring success. As for the bar itself, well, it's all about having a good time at the end of the day. I'll drink to that.

RUPERT CLEVELY

Just Don't Call it a Gastro Pub

Rupert Clevely said goodbye to a six-figure salary when he started his pub business and nearly paid the price when the chain ran into financial crisis a few years later. He took another look at the figures, jiggled his priorities and hasn't looked back since. Today the £25m turnover Geronimo Inns group is firing on all cylinders, with growth its main priority.

Right down to the toilets

"I hate the term 'gastro pub'," Rupert Clevely complains over his bowl of salad. I've gone for steak and chips, and I allow him to elaborate as I concentrate on the food. "It sounds ghastly. I mean, what does it stand for? We're just a bunch of nice pubs with good food, that's what we are," he says, gesturing with his fork.

Unfortunately for Clevely, the set-up at Geronimo Inns fits squarely into the popular gastro mould. Each of the 27 boozers is thoughtfully put together with kitsch furniture and decorative accents in abundance. There is a good choice of ales and wines and the food has earned its fair share of Michelin ratings.

The Phoenix Pub, just off the King's Road in Chelsea, is the setting for our meeting and it reflects the Geronimo template down to the toilets.

I can't give you a diner's review of the service. As a waiter you are unlikely to give sloppy treatment to the owner of your restaurant, less likely still if he's sitting opposite a journalist. But I can vouch for the set-up and the atmosphere (Jo, Rupert's wife's, responsibility), which are intrinsic to the chain's popularity.

From corporate man to publican

The Clevelys founded Geronimo along with a third partner in 1995. Disillusioned with his cushy, well-paid marketing job with super-brand champagne Veuve Clicquot, Rupert extended the mortgage on his flat to buy a pub called the Chelsea Ram in south-west London.

"My idea was to make grotty pubs really nice," explains Clevely, summing up his strategy for improving life for London's drinkers in the mid-1990s.

But for several years he worked only part-time on the business, reluctant to sever the safety net of a salary from Clicquot.

The spruced-up pub was an instant success, increasing weekly takings by 700% in a few short months. But it was not until a third pub was up and running that Clevely finally cut the umbilical cord of his employer and went into business full-time.

"I remember sitting at home and thinking, 'I've got one or two pubs that are going really well, why can't we go ahead and do this again and roll it out? Where am I going to be in five years' time otherwise? I'm going to be working for Clicquot. I'll be 43; I'll still be earning £100,000 a year or maybe a bit more.'

"At any stage they could come to me and say 'You're not the right guy, we don't want you any more, we're making redundancies in the business', and what am I going to do then? Why don't I do it now when I haven't got as big overheads as I would have in the future?"

Problems with the local mafia...

Upon his resignation Clevely demanded a greater share of the firm from his business partner who he felt contributed less to its development. Knowing this "wouldn't go down too well" the trio opted to split the business, with the Clevelys taking on two less profitable pubs and the partner walking away with the Ram.

Now as a husband-and-wife team they chose to develop the business and sold 15% of their equity to fund an expansion plan, which helped them acquire a further ten pubs in the space of five years. But growth came at a price and the business became overstretched as the financial pressures of running a major London chain began to sink in.

At the same time one of the acquired pubs located in the East End became a particularly sharp thorn in the business' side. It was Clevely's first experience of losing money and interest from local organised criminals did nothing to sweeten the experience.

He recollects: "We had a pub in the East End which was awful. We had problems with local mafia and we had ghastly moments sitting behind the bar and guys standing at the door with guns in their pockets. That wasn't a good time at all.

"In the end we gave that pub to the mafia. One of the biggest mistakes that you can make is not to cut your losses. When you buy a site and develop it, you'll know very quickly whether that site is going to work and if it doesn't work, you've got to accept that, cut it and move on."

Development at the rate of knots

The problems meant that the lion's share of the hundreds of thousands of pounds ploughed into the Geronimo from the equity sale went towards shoring up the business and not to growing it as had been planned.

Clevely learned his lesson and became choosier about his acquisitions, but the experience hasn't stopped him developing the business at a rate of knots. Having bought out his initial investors and brought in tens of millions of pounds in new money, the publican has gone on an unprecedented shopping spree.

In late 2006 it took on a funding package worth £24.5m, composed of £10m in equity money and an extended loan facility from the bank. Clevely says the cash flushed into the business will see it reach 30 outlets in total.

Most recently it went towards the purchase of six pubs in London (all Geronimo pubs are in the UK capital), formally owned by Punch Taverns. The deal was reportedly worth between £8m and £9m and Clevely now owns 12 valuable freeholds as well as 15 pub licences.

Readying to sell

He is unashamedly candid about his intentions for the business, which are to increase its value by as much as possible before selling it when the economy picks up again. That could be very soon, or it could be years away in the misty future.

"We're three years into our plan and we might have thought two or three years ago that we'd like to sell it. The reality is that with the current market it's not viable for us to sell it. So therefore we might be five or six years from the original date. That's the key, I think, to be flexible but to have a goal.

"It might be a year off, it might be two years, but in the next three years we need to think about what we're going to do, because this business can't just go on and grow and grow through acquiring freehold sites.

"I don't want to be here in the next 20 years. I'm not going to pass this on down to my daughters. I want to make some money out of it and then I want to relax a bit more because I left school at 17 and have been working every day since then, apart from holidays. So that's quite important to me."

Sky's the limit

So what's Rupert's formula for a great pub? "A relaxed atmosphere," sure; "good food and drink," of course; "…and Sky TV." Eh? I heard him correctly. He reckons that sport is such an integral part of people's lives – men and women – that it has a place even in a gastr…I mean upmarket chain of pubs.

You need to strike a balance, of course. Clevely has no plans to introduce projector TVs and loud speakers, but international cricket, the odd game of rugby or even, on selected evenings, a big football match can complement even the most salubrious surroundings.

"When I go to the pub I want it to be an extension of my home. If I can't afford Sky, because I'm not going to give them £35 a month, I'll go to my pub and if they don't have it, well I'm going to the pub down the road instead! That's the key – it's an extension of your home."

MAX CLIFFORD

The Tabloids' Chief Go-to Man

Max Clifford needs no introduction – mainly because that is his job and he's exceptionally good at it. Britain's top PR man is also the industry's lone celebrity, a status he achieved through a serendipitous collision of events early in his career.

"You just have to stand there and be the mouth"

"Can you make anyone famous? Of course you can," declares Max Clifford as he reclines baron-like in an executive throne behind an imposing glass desk at his headquarters in London. "You just have to know which doors to knock on."

"You're a journalist and business is your beat," he reminds me. "So, next week you would reveal that Lord Sugar is about to go bust." I gasp. "He's not, it's make-believe, but if he was I would know. You'd break the story and I'd arrange interviews with television, radio and newspapers worldwide.

"I have people coming to me all the time with some really sensational stuff. I'd get on to *Panorama* and say 'Give this guy a chance; he'll break two or three big stories in the next few months'. You just have to stand there and be the mouth." I like this idea. "Our fees start at £15,000 a month," he adds. My smile fades.

Many long-term clients pay considerably more than those mere pennies for Mr Clifford to manage their media profile, but as Max points out a good slice of the people he represents want news about them strangled, not liberated.

Undoing a Ratner

Examples of people who made it onto Clifford's books include Gerald Ratner, the jewellery magnate who famously crashed his businesses by commenting publicly that his products were cheap because they were "crap". Years after this disaster he came up with an idea for an online jewellery business and asked Clifford to handle the PR around it.

"The problem he faced was he denied that he'd said it the way the papers wrote it and he kept protesting his innocence. Well no journalist is going to write that, so I said put your hands up and admit it, get past it and say, 'By the way, look what I'm up to now'."

It worked. A *Telegraph* headline dated December 2003 gushes 'Ratner Sparkles in Online Jewellery', meanwhile a *Times* article confirms that the 'King of Diamonds Deals Again'. They both mention his foot-in-mouth moment – the best PR man in the world couldn't stifle that – but the focus in both cases is on the entrepreneur's rebirth.

Well, it's good PR

Being invited to Max Clifford Associates is a surreal, dream-like experience. The place is decorated sparingly in white. There is a gaggle of PR girls, chiefly blonde and in their twenties. As I enter, a grinning Chris Eubank passes me in the doorway, and when I find a chair it is opposite wide-eyed Big Brother star Sophie Reade.

The oddities don't let up when you're inside Clifford's corner room, which is covered in greeting cards thanking him for jobs well done and the charity work which occupies much of his time. The walls are adorned with faded tabloid covers screaming 'Freddie Starr Ate My Hamster', 'Mellor Made Love in Chelsea Strip' and 'Beckham's Secret Affair'.

The PR man is proud of these outrageous headlines, which are some of the most famous in newspaper history. This despite, as I put it to him, the fact that most of them are made up. Clifford is philosophical about the fact-to-fiction ratio of his clients' stories. In many cases he denies the story, but the editors run it anyway.

Pointing at the Freddie Starr front page, he reflects: "I said to the editor of *The Sun*, 'Look he denies this', and he said 'Okay, but will you sue us if we run with it?' I said 'No, because we think it's good PR.' Fortunately we were right."

He guessed that few would believe the story but that it would chime with Starr's zany act and appeal to his growing fan base. "We had great exposure that everyone was laughing at. His tour sold out and they added another 100 dates. That's 25 years ago and people still remember it – I can't think of a more famous headline."

Building a reputation

Asked how he developed his reputation as a go-to man for people with media quandaries, Clifford shrugs his shoulders. "I honestly don't know how I came to be in this position. Right place and right time I suppose."

The facts speak for themselves. Clifford landed a job in the press office of record label EMI in 1962 and was soon given a role promoting an emerging band called 'The Beatles'. He admits his role in their success was "non-existent", but being associated with such a monster act opened plenty of doors.

Being one of three youngsters in the press team, Clifford was handed a clutch of new artists and musicians by more senior members of the team who were busy working with stars from the 50s era. It linked him to huge names that developed in the brave new world of 1960s Britain.

"There was no such thing as PR in those days. When Sid [Gillingham, a senior press officer at EMI] decided to start his own music promotions business he took me with him," he explains, leaning forward in his chair with a squeak. "He continued working with the older guys so I dealt with the new blood."

When Gillingham decided to return to his old career as a journalist, a 27-year-old Clifford struck out on his own, retaining the custom of notable names. Having already worked with Jimi Hendrix, Joe Cocker and Bob Dylan, to name a few, he was in a strong position to develop the business.

The rest is history, or so he tells it. Clifford's story from that day to this is one of seizing opportunities and, having landed them, doing a good enough job to get recommendations and referrals. Being a figurehead for the business helps too, although not all PR professionals agree.

"My personal brand is very important to my business. It means I never have to pitch for business and I can pick the people and businesses I want to work with. I don't want to sound arrogant; it just helps if people come to you first."

At 66 retirement is still a long way off for Clifford, who thoroughly enjoys his job. Whether it's a charity golf tournament in Spain or spilling the beans on a kiss-and-tell story, he relishes the work. It's partly because his finely tuned method of promotion so often mixes fun events and celebrity endorsements with serious goals.

"I never had a plan, it was just one door opened and then another one opened and I realised if you had stars you could promote anything: a clothing range, a hotel, a restaurant or a charity," he says, as if it's the simplest thing in the world.

MARK CONSTANTINE

The Cosmetic Industry's Very Own Willy Wonka

Lush Cosmetics picked up where The Body Shop left off on the UK high street, and with its range of colourful soaps, perfumes and bath-time tomfoolery it has developed into an international business of 650 shops, with a turnover of more than £150m. Now co-founder Mark Constantine wants Lush to save the world.

Sweets, treats and rotating roles

Lush's Poole-based laboratory is an exploding melee of concoctions created in big frothing vats with ingredients ranging from cocoa powder to nettles to Shea butter (the natural fat obtained from the fruit of the African Karite tree, for those of you who didn't know). I half expect to see a river of chocolate and some Oompa-Loompas filing past.

Indeed, enter any of the UK's 90-odd Lush shops and you would be forgiven if your first inclination was to dribble. So much of the product sounds edible – with chocolate, marshmallow and honey included – that the effect is oddly confectionary-like. And yet people seem to dig it. Basically, the message is: bath-time is fun. And it seems to be a popular message.

The business itself is run in a fairly slapdash way, though perhaps not as chaotically if Wonka himself was pulling the strings. The senior team have no fixed roles or titles and they rotate responsibilities; there is no marketing or advertising budget (although they do have a PR team) and international travel is restricted because of the company's stance on the environment.

Mark Constantine is the personification of this system. He is unable to recall the most basic facts about the business, including in what year it was founded (1994). Even weirder, he has to ask a colleague how many shops he owns. When I ask him to clarify Lush's turnover he gestures vaguely: "Erm, about *that*." Then I'm pointed to the press office for clarification.

Losing everything...

A mission statement on the website reads, "We believe in long baths, sharing showers, filling the world with perfume and the right to make mistakes, lose everything and start again". The seemingly incongruous second half of the sentence refers to Lush's own troubled past. Taken as a whole it's a passable summary of Constantine's life.

Actually the losing everything bit is a white lie. When the team who eventually created Lush were on their second business, a mail-order cosmetics company called Cosmetics to Go, they did lose millions, but they retained 10,000 formulas, the loyalty of their suppliers and the wherewithal to start again.

All except for Constantine: "There's some statistic about people going bust: some big number either have a heart attack or a breakdown so it must be a fairly big strain. I avoided both but it wasn't a great time.

"I wouldn't have started again if it hadn't been for my colleagues. I really didn't feel like picking myself up at all. Then people I had worked with kept popping round and they finally got me going again. To be honest, I was grateful that they were still interested in working with me."

Cosmetics to Go had been a roaring success, but it suffered from a fundamental problem: the company lost a pound on every product it sold. In a collapse reminiscent of the dotcom bust (though it predated that event by at least six years) the business built up a huge fan base and healthy demand, before promptly running out of money.

The nail in the coffin hit home when, already hamstrung by cash-flow troubles, the company's control centre flooded. A botched radiator removal job on the top floor meant that when the office cleared late one Christmas Eve, a thermostat opened and water poured from an exposed pipe for two days.

The team were called into work when a passer-by reported seeing water streaming out from under the front door. Insurers refused to pay for the damaged computer and phone equipment and the company was sunk. The episode sticks in the mind of Constantine, who had to make 200 people redundant that day.

Starting again

When Constantine started for a third time in 1994, now with a group of "five or six" co-founders from his previous businesses (his first was Constantine & Weir, which sold its intellectual property rights to The Body Shop for £9m), the fledgling Lush operation was financed through new mortgages, selling houses, car-boot sales and maxed-out credit cards.

They even sold items that the receivers from Cosmetics to Go left behind, including scraps of old material. The desks and chairs still had 'for sale' labels on them and Constantine deliberately kept his for five years as a reminder of how things can go dramatically wrong.

But the vastly experienced team had learned lessons from the two very different episodes and within six months they had secured investment from a couple of business angels and opened the first Lush shop.

"It was a big collaboration of people, some of whom were prepared to work for nothing. We were successful because teamwork is the key – everything else is irrelevant.

"It went like a rocket in the beginning and we were saying 'no' to more people than we were saying 'yes' to. Lots of people wanted to partner, to invest or open a shop for us. There was a lot of interest and it was down to us to pick through that and make the right decisions."

Constantine set a target of opening 1000 shops and with the current rate approaching 100 a year, that should be reached soon. After consulting his partner, Andrew Gerrie, he estimates the team own "about 500" of the 650 branches opened so far. The rest are run by territory licensees, notably in Russia, and there are "between ten and 20" franchises.

Green and clean

In the last few years the company has come out as a staunch backer of green causes ("We always had the values but we only made it known in the last few years," he admits), and I put it to Constantine that such a large firm must do its fair share of damage to the environment.

His answer is creditably honest: "Consumerism is by its nature not very environmental, but people are going to consume anyway and what I need to ask is can I create something better and cleaner than my competitors? All we can do is try to set an example and hope the market follows.

"The lovely thing about green business is it's the same as running a business really well: cutting your costs, eliminating waste, dropping energy bills, reducing packaging, insulating buildings – all of those things have a positive impact on the bottom line as well as the world around us.

"The difference is if you employ a team of accountants and you ask them to cut costs, everyone hates them and joins your competitors. If you have a team of people who are passionate about those ethics they are very happy to do all of that and it doesn't piss them off."

MICHELLE DEWBERRY

The Apprentice's IT Girl

From checkout girl to TV star and beyond, Michelle Dewberry has enjoyed a rollercoaster existence in her young life. She describes why *The Apprentice* was only the beginning and how being an entrepreneur beats employment – even with Alan Sugar – hands down.

Tragic turning point

At the age of 18, Michelle Dewberry accepted her first job, with a £7000 salary attached. Eight years later, when she was victorious in the second series of TV's *The Apprentice*, the £100,000-a-year prize job with (the then-'Sir') Alan Sugar represented a near-50% pay cut.

The most remarkable part of Dewberry's rise to business stardom is nothing to do with television and everything to do with the rags-to-riches tale that preceded it. Growing up in meagre surroundings in Hull, she spent time in care, left school before she was 16 and suffered at the hands of an abusive father.

The decisive moment in Dewberry's life was also her lowest ebb when, at the age of 17, her 19-year-old sister was killed in a tragic accident. Since leaving school the teenage Dewberry had wandered without direction from one menial job to another, but the event inspired her to plot a course for a meaningful career.

"When she died I made a pact with myself that I was going to turn my life around. She died just before she started a college course and it made me realise that people put things off – I realised I had to get some qualifications."

The decision kicked off a chain of events (helped by fortitude and bare-faced cheek) that propelled Dewberry to a £185,000 consulting job with a major European telecoms company. By the time she was 24 she was being offered further pay rises and director-level positions at the firm.

Pink cardboard and business basics

"I'm a very goal-driven person. Everything about me is ticking boxes. I've had plans with my life since I was 17 – almost on a day-to-day basis," she says.

"My first goal was to earn £12,000 a year. I thought I would be so rich! Then I made it my goal to buy my first house by the time I was 21. I would do stuff like babysitting and get paid in tea towels and cutlery. I had it all under my bed at home, all this stuff ready for when I moved out."

Dewberry earned herself two NVQ qualifications and won an apprenticeship with the Saint John Ambulance service. Her first mentors taught her the business fundamentals, like not to use bad language in job interviews – the sort of lessons a basic education would have given her.

On one occasion, before applying to work at Miss Selfridge, Dewberry asked shop workers how they had succeeded in finding work: "They said 'Make your CV stand out'. So I wrote my application on fluorescent pink cardboard – it was months before I realised that wasn't what they had meant."

Art of persuasion, fruits of perseverance

Learning from this experience and others like it, she won a place as an admin girl in the IT department of a local company called Kingston Communications. True to form, she had applied for a managerial role, but was refused because of her glaring lack of experience.

Unperturbed, Dewberry set about looking for a path up the career ladder. She convinced her superiors to pay for her to take an IT course, and when she failed the exam, bribed the receptionist to let her take it again straightaway, passing second time round. "I've still got both results saying 'pass' and 'fail'. The difference is determination," she beams.

She persuaded Kingston to give her a job as a network analyst, looking after the company's IT infrastructure...and immediately began looking for the next opportunity: "As part of the deal I still had to do my admin job, so when I was serving tea in meetings I'd do it really slowly so I could eavesdrop on what was going on," she giggles.

Through her clandestine activities, Dewberry learned that a problem had developed between Kingston and one of its major clients, Tiscali. She began scratching around for information about the breakdown and wrote a paper describing how it could be resolved. She mailed it to the client as well as her own superiors, risking disciplinary action.

What she got was a promotion to lead the relationship between the two firms. When eventually she left Kingston, Tiscali got in contact complaining that the relationship had broken down again and asking if she would take over the job in-house.

She describes saving the business millions on operational costs by consolidating its IT systems, but only being paid "about 38 grand". Other companies could surely use the same service and would pay considerably more to a freelance contractor than she was earning as an employee. She decided to strike out alone.

From freelance to Brentwood

"I researched the freelance market and went off and got some phenomenal contracts. My biggest was working for Colt Telecom earning £185,000 when I was 24. They said they wanted to keep me on as a director in their organisation – I didn't know what to do. It frightened me. It was a phenomenal position for a 24-year-old: a senior director in a humungous European telecoms company."

It was while juggling the decision whether to return to salaried employment or stay as an independent contractor that Dewberry received a tip-off about *The Apprentice*. At the time she knew nothing about the show and very little about 'Suralan' himself.

"With *The Apprentice* I was offered something which was off the Richter scale in terms of extraordinariness. It wasn't that I loved Alan Sugar or desperately wanted to go and work in Brentwood; I thought if I can get *here*, just me, how much more successful could I be if I had an amazing entrepreneur take me under his wing?"

And so it turned out. Dewberry revelled in the weekly challenges, learning experiences with (the now) Lord Sugar, the camaraderie and ultimately the victory. What she didn't sign up for was the fame, which nearly cost her her sanity, especially when an off-screen affair with fellow contestant Syed Ahmed went public.

Dewberry left employment with the Sugar business empire after just a few months. Harangued by paparazzi, she went into hiding. She dyed her hair black as a rudimentary disguise and went to ground, waiting until her front-page status lost its lustre and the press lost their appetite.

"I wouldn't go out and I missed out on a lot of opportunities – I wasn't in the right place for them. I can't complain though, having gone on TV. I just wish I was better prepared and perhaps better supported during that time."

Entrepreneurial, not an entrepreneur

Now at the ripe old age of 30 and with a wealth of varied experiences under her belt, she has once again struck out on her own. This time with her own business: fashion and lifestyle website, Chiconomise.

The idea behind the project is to provide trend-conscious young females with a host of daily deals on clothes, accessories, leisure pursuits and holidays. Launched in 2009 the business is just getting off the ground, but having shuffled her business plan a few times already, Dewberry feels she is on track.

"I'm not an entrepreneur," she says. "That's someone who has successfully created and exited a business. I am entrepreneurial; I feel a bit of a w*nker saying I'm an entrepreneur. I'm just somebody who wants to be in charge of their own destiny."

Sir Tom Farmer

Britain's Richest Mechanic

Sir Tom Farmer is the world's most successful mechanic, having earned the bulk of a reported £120m fortune from the sale of the Kwik-Fit chain during the late 1990s. But he is more than a trumped-up tyre salesman, with businesses encompassing sport, photo processing and, most peculiarly, island ownership.

"I keep thinking I'll wake up and all this has been a dream"

A child of the 1940s, Farmer had plenty of time to form a list of business dos and don'ts and he rattles them off in our interview as if reading from a script. He knows Kwik-Fit's narrative too, having presented the story to eager crowds of grass-root entrepreneurs for decades.

"I keep thinking I'll wake up and all this has been a dream," says a thoughtful Farmer. "It's incredible how my life has turned out. I keep thinking I'll wake up tomorrow and be 21 years of age, driving a van and delivering tyres," he smiles, alluding to his beginnings in the car parts industry.

He explains that this wouldn't be a bad thing. His is no rags-to-riches story and while his upbringing was modest he enjoyed a supportive family environment and the confidence that comes with being the youngest of seven siblings.

Trust and service

Farmer's reliance on those around him stemmed from his cohesive upbringing and his early experiences of work. Upon being promoted to van driver at the tyre depot, the 18-year-old entrepreneur-to-be was hauled into his manager's office.

"They were great mentors and they told me exactly what they wanted from me. On my first day they asked me to describe the new job. I said I was going to be a driver. They said you're not and we want you to remember this: you're a *representative* of our organisation."

As the only point of contact between the business and the majority of its customers in the area, Farmer became a mobile advocate for the business. The van, uniform, presentation and communication were all on behalf of his employer and they wanted him to know it.

Five years later, when Farmer invested £200 to start his own tyre depot, he transferred the values of trust and service – but not before he got the thing up and running: "At that time it was illegal to sell tyres or anything else at a discount. If you went off the manufacturer's price list you'd be taken to court and fined. It was anti-competitive," he states. "But the law was just changing, so discounters were popping up. I opened up a shop in Edinburgh, which did all right.

"Then one day a local newspaper decided to write an article about me; a young lad starting a business selling tyres at discount prices. I exaggerated slightly because they asked me, 'Who supplies you? They could get into trouble!' I told them how I needed to get in my van in the middle of the night and meet people in dark lay-bys," he chuckles.

"A couple of weeks later one of the Sunday papers dropped through the letterbox and the headline in the front page read 'Tyre King Tommy'. That particular Sunday there were 42 cars outside my business when I got to work. It never stopped from that moment."

Eventually it went public at eight shillings a share and six weeks later the price rocketed in value to 126 shillings. In no time the company was subject of takeover bids and agreeing to sell to a US company for £450,000 – about £8m in today's money. The 28-year-old businessman retired to America.

But inactivity suited neither Farmer nor his spouse: "One evening I went to dinner with my wife. She took my hand over the dinner table and told me she loved me and said she married me for better or worse, but not to live with me 24 hours a day and seven days a week. We had to do something about it!"

Reuniting with his old pals in an Edinburgh pub, Farmer outlined a new business venture specialising in exhausts. Such niche outfits were popular in the US but were yet to gain traction in the UK. In 1971, Kwik-Fit was created. He devised the name from the old, deliberately misspelled, newspaper ads he wrote to promote his teenage odd-jobs service.

"Shareholders are number four, though they don't like it"

As a customer-facing business, Kwik-Fit relied on good people ("we hired people not employees," he tells me) and Farmer ranks them above customers, suppliers and shareholders in his list of priorities; for without good people you won't get sales and without sales investors will steer clear.

The hierarchy continues in a logical progression: "Number two on the list is suppliers, because if you don't have dependable suppliers you won't have anything for number one [staff] to sell. If you get those two right and a product people want to buy, then you have a business.

"That basically means you have the right ingredients to sell to number three, who is the customer, and if they are happy, you've got everything you need to make shareholders happy. They're number four; though they don't often like being told so."

His system explains the "You can't get better than a Kwik-Fit fitter" slogan and the dancing mechanics who feature in the company's memorable TV advertising. Like the RAC's 'Knights of the Road', the slogan had a dual benefit of reassuring customers and making shop workers feel proud of their jobs.

Soon Kwik-Fit was also approached by investors and again Farmer agreed to sell his stake, only this time he retained a seat on the board of directors. I was only with them a short while before the board had a big falling out and I decided to leave, but in the fullness of time I ended up buying out the other directors. I sold off all the other businesses apart from the parts shop in Holland and merged it into the Kwik-Fit brand."

Quickly acquiring two further businesses, including one which had absorbed his first tyre depot some years earlier, Farmer transformed Kwik-Fit from a national firm with 200 shops into a multi-national chain employing 12,000 people. He sold it to Ford in 1999 for £1bn, earning him a £75m windfall.

A knighthood, a football club and an island

Since selling, Sir Tom has engaged in extensive charity work. He's also bought a 90% stake in Edinburgh's Hibernian Football Club, after financial problems made it likely that the team would be absorbed by local rivals Hearts. (He isn't a football fan, though.) Even more adventurous, he bought the 65-acre island of Inchkeith in the Firth of Forth, because a friend dared him to.

Last but not least in Sir Tom's amusing list of odd spending decisions was his £100,000 grant to the Scottish National Party to fund their campaign for the 2007 Scottish Parliament's general election. While a proud Scot, he is not a nationalist.

Noting that devolution seemed to be having little impact in Scotland and witnessing the frustration expressed by many of his countrymen, Farmer decided to give the process a nudge: "I thought if I stood up and was counted, other people would follow – and that's what happened.

"I want a Scotland that is more independent but not separate; my children are independent from my wife and I, and they stand on their own two feet," he analogises. "They look after their own affairs, generate their own income and so on, but they are not separate from us."

ANTHONY GANJOU

An Advertising Natural

Curb is a pioneering advertising business that uses natural, sustainable resources to create stunning and unusual campaigns for its growing client base. Founder Anthony Ganjou is a young entrepreneur still in the early stages of his career, but so far he's been making all the right moves – applying unusual techniques to age-old needs, and revolutionising hi-tech advertising by going all-out low-tech and natural.

Eyeballs

Into the precise and accountable market of modern advertising – with video, pay-per-click, social media and all the rest– entrepreneur Anthony Ganjou has launched Curb, an advertising agency that proposes to build brands using sand sculptures, snow tags and crop circles. His idea is out of step with digital modernity but he reckons that's why it's going to work.

"The odd thing about society is that we're all programmed to expect where we see nature – where nature fits," says Ganjou. "But at Curb we put nature in contexts where you don't expect it," which makes it, he says, "incredibly effective" as an advertising medium. "Ultimately as every advertiser knows, it's all about getting eyeballs on the message and that's what we do, first and foremost."

Though Curb is barely a year old when we meet, it has made a running start. In no time the company has put together a client base that much older agencies would envy, and counts the BBC, Condé Nast, Budweiser, Kia and Royal Mail among its customers. Turnover was expected to top £250,000 in year one and Ganjou wanted to quadruple that in 2010.

"We know there is a niche now; there is clearly a demand for effective, genuinely green and sustainable media platforms," says the t-shirted entrepreneur as he sips from his glass of water. "There were a lot of consultancies out there who were saying you could better your footprint by using less paper and change your font and all that, but there was no real central point for creativity and innovation that would work in a media capacity – that's when Curb was born." As if to underline his point he passes me a carving of a figure etched into a flat rectangle slab of wood. The detail is impressive and I can see how it would attract advertisers with an eye for the unusual – then he tells me the artist burnt the image into his 'canvas' using only the sun's rays and a magnifying glass.

Other feats of advertising sorcery achieved by Curb are equally impressive: a 100-metre long message raked into Blackpool beach; detailed faces and model buildings sculpted from compost; and the Mona Lisa recreated by manipulating dirt on a car's rear windscreen.

Canny with costs

Even the old-fashioned alternative advert approach can still be fruitful alongside these bold innovations.

"People have been doing sand sculpting and big adverts in fields for 20 years, but they still make the national press. So there's a certain amount of historical evidence that shows that people don't get desensitised to it," says Ganjou.

"The medium is much cheaper and more eye-catching than someone seeing a van or a billboard. It's the same thing with the snow-tagging. Although it's not as relevant in London because it doesn't snow as much, it allows us to brand every single major ski resort around the world for free."

I ask if something like sea-tagging is strictly legal, given that there are designated areas for outdoor promotions. "What are they going to do? Call the police?" he shoots back. "By the time the police get there it will have evaporated."

An agency for agencies – or being canny with competition, too

Clearly, Curb is as shrewd as it is creative – and this is reflected in their business strategy as well as their artistic work. Ganjou has structured the business as an 'agency for agencies' so as not to position it as a competitor to the established marketing industry. Much of his business is done through intermediaries who want to impress their clients with innovative and environmentally responsible campaigns.

The business gets a lot of its new projects through referrals, therefore, and hasn't needed to pitch for business recently. The added benefit of creating such unique and eye-catching displays is that they advertise Curb's services as much as they do the client's.

For the artists that do the work, Curb is a medium through which they can express themselves and earn some money for their efforts. Some are business-people in their own right while others are downright hippies. Either way, picking the best suppliers was a key factor for Ganjou when he set up the business.

"It's a minefield out there for agencies that want to do something like this to know whether the artist is going to turn up or get drunk the night before and be hungover and create something rubbish," he laughs.

"Ultimately the people we work with are amazing with what they do which is delivery. They're not necessarily brilliant at marketing and sales, so what we do is help them attract business, so they can do what they do best."

Though it started trading in September 2008, Ganjou spent the first part of that year sourcing artists for the business and developing terms of work with them. It meant Curb launched with a full suite of services and could pitch to big companies with a varied portfolio of visual displays.

Growing the business

Curb's first sale was to a friend who runs a hotel chain which at the time was re-launching its website. Partly as a favour he persuaded his friend to trial the 'clean adverts' – subsequently adopted by Kia, Nicorette and eparktennis.com – and created "a huge amount of buzz" for the brand.

What followed was a period of cold calling agencies for new business. A spontaneous campaign of snow-tagging in February 2009 developed huge coverage for Extreme, which approved the displays at short notice when snow descended on London, but also for Curb. "We still regularly get people who say, 'you're the guys that did the snow stuff'," he beams. "So that was really the catalyst."

All well and good, but in this era of demonstrable returns don't clients wonder whether people are appreciating their message or just looking at the pretty pictures? As attractive and exciting as Curb's work is, it's not as certain to win you sales as a Google ad.

"I think that what the client cares about is getting bang for their buck and we are a company that delivers effectiveness and return on investment on budgets first and foremost. That it's sustainable and green is almost a secondary factor.

"As for return on our investment, we're obviously extremely keen to work to understand how the campaigns have ultimately affected clients' bottom lines. They tell us what the impact of the campaign has been, because they want to shout about it, because they get the added PR and publicity from it."

Of course, most big brands advertise across media in campaigns that range from the cold calculation of 'pay per click' to the opulent warmth of mere creative display. With that in mind and Curb's first-mover advantage secured, Ganjou's audacious 400% year-on-year growth estimates don't sound quite so cuckoo after all.

DAWN GIBBINS MBE

Flooring the Competition

Dawn Gibbins is flying the flag for women in what can be seen as a man's world. But having co-founded, developed and sold a manufacturing company, that supposedly most masculine of businesses, Gibbins is allowing feminine influences into her work. Now she's on a mission to make floors – yes floors – sexy.

"Don't be daft, you're going into business with Dawn!"

On first impressions you would be forgiven for concluding that Dawn Gibbins is mad as a box of frogs – over the years she has developed a reputation for wild eccentricity, and seems keen on maintaining it.

Since exiting Flowcrete, the business she started with her inventor father Peter, she has launched a campaign to convert homeowners to barefoot living, which she argues is much healthier than walking around in shoes. She is an unswerving believer in *feng shui* and as a side project has volunteered to help rebrand the Cheshire town of Congleton. In short, Gibbins is having a lot of fun.

I meet her on a warm afternoon in late summer. She is in London to give a talk on the psychology of selling your business, organised by Coutts & Co bank. Her husband, Mark Grieves, who is managing director of Dawn's old business Flowcrete, is in town to pick up a Queen's Award for Enterprise.

A little late, Gibbins whirls in with flowing summer dress, flip-flops, beads and big earrings, oblivious to the surroundings of our meeting near Buckingham Palace, and offers me an enthusiastic 'hello'. Our chat takes twice as long as an average interview. The conversation is ten to the dozen and Gibbins delivers her points in a blur of enthusiastic hand gestures. She fidgets, reaches out and touches my arm more than once to ensure my full attention and regularly finishes sentences with a nod and a 'yeah', as if an alter-ego is in agreement with her.

"I'm the daughter of a great inventor who designed seamless flooring; a clever style of flooring using liquid resins instead of tiles or boards," Gibbins starts to explain. "In the early eighties my father designed a solution for Mars which prevented sugar corroding the floor in their factories.

"He was about to sell the solution for £2,000, and he'd been doing this sort of thing all the time, but my mum finally flipped and said, 'Don't be daft you're going into business with Dawn'. We set up Flowcrete in 1982 and developed a line of floor solutions using his inventions to fit our clients' needs." That was how it all began.

Flooring it

With its emphasis on research and development the business grew quickly and it pioneered a host of breakthrough flooring innovations for the healthcare, military and leisure sectors. To you and I, a floor is something you walk on, but Peter Gibbins came up with floors that reduce lighting bills, fight superbugs in hospitals and act as camouflage against aerial threats.

"We managed to make a profit year-on-year even though it was through new products every time. Our turnover went up from £40,000 in the first year to £150,000 and then £300,000 in year three.

"It was ticking along nicely making money here and there – all done ad-hoc and on the fly – until about eight years in when I decided I wanted to go and get educated, so I signed up for lots of short courses on growing companies and being a woman in business, and I basically learned how you were really supposed to run a business. It was great.

"I'm embarrassed to say this but around the same time we wrote our first business plan; lo and behold, this was when growth really started accelerating. When we all had our ambitions aligned and we knew where we wanted to go and how to get there, it was the catalyst of our growth curve."

So it was that ten years later Dawn Gibbins began to accumulate her stockpile of entrepreneurial awards. The business had developed a stellar cast of customers, including airports, car manufacturers and military organisations, turnover was in multiples of millions and profits developed year-on-year.

The poisoned chalice and the corporate detox

But then disaster struck: "If you're not careful, winning an award like the Veuve Clicquot can be a poisoned chalice. Someone told me that at the time and I thought 'how stupid', because I was raring to go, but you get all that publicity, you get in-demand, you're on a high and you become distracted.

"In the year after (2004) the business didn't do well at all, in fact we made our first ever loss."

Stunned by the sudden decline of Flowcrete, Gibbins sct about turning the company around. By 2004 it was turning over £20m and had a vast array of products and brands which baffled customers as well as staff. Realising that Flowcrete had become too complex, Gibbins embarked on a course of simplification, which she labelled its "corporate detox".

"We'd done so many acquisitions, and brought so many new products to the market that our people were just saying, 'Who are we? Where are we going?'. Being told that by a team of 50 is a bit shocking so we thought we'd better do what they say. We started by rationalising the product range and halved it to 50."

A survey of employees around the same time returned a satisfaction rate of only 65%. Salvaging Flowcrete employees' battered morale quickly became priority number one for the management team and Gibbins resolved to introduce a whole raft of measures that would restore workers' faith in the business.

"We had to clearly write down the mission statement and communicate it to everyone, not only for the group but for each individual country. We introduced a newsletter – *Our World* – and something called 'Performing with Pam', which was our performance every month; how we were doing in every part of the world.

"Also we set up incentive schemes, which I think was a really good [development] because we got everybody to watch the bottom line. Nobody got a bonus that year because we lost money so we said, 'If we do a bottom line, your bonus will be linked to it'. We turned it into a competition to see who could perform the best.

"The survey really hurt. It was all confidential so people could say what they like. Me and a couple of the directors harmonised the results and we published them. If you've got openness and sharing, you can do something to improve the company. Two years later we had an approval rating of 80% and turnover of £36m."

No rest for the wicked

When Gibbins finally sold the business for a reported £30m in 2008, she, like all accomplished entrepreneurs, suddenly became wealthy. Yet she immediately set about constructing a new company, Barefoot Living, instead of retiring and kicking back.

The business is aimed squarely at the female market, which she expects to develop new spending power in the next ten years. Meanwhile it is drawing on scientific studies suggesting that walking barefoot is good for you to create a portfolio of floor products that are pleasing to the eye and to the touch.

"'Lose the shoes' is our strap-line. We are a barefoot office and our showroom is barefoot too so you really do have to take your shoes off."

Gibbins was recently awarded an MBE for her services to industry, but she plans to create plenty more waves before she quits.

DAVID GOLD

From Buttons to West Ham

From selling buttons to passers-by as a means of surviving post-war London to running a company portfolio valued at half-a-billion pounds, David Gold has experienced just about everything the world of enterprise has to offer. Now in his seventies Gold's priority is succession planning, but he can't resist a last roll of the dice.

Lower pay than the tea lady

Gold has told his story to hundreds of journalists over the years, but despite his busy schedule he is eager to talk. Last night he retuned from Birmingham City FC in his gleaming Jaguar saloon, he tells me; this morning he was at a board meeting at Ann Summers' headquarters; tomorrow he'll be flying his helicopter back to Birmingham to meet some new players and chat with the manager.

On the day our interview takes place at his huge Surrey estate, these are Gold's two main business interests: the football club he sold to foreign investors later in the year and the £100m-plus turnover sex shop chain run by his daughters. CEO Jacqueline is now as famous as her father, yet when she started working in the shops in 1979 he paid her less than the tea lady.

Gold delivers his sentences with a grin and clearly enjoys sprinkling in the odd quip, which is more often than not self-deprecating. Perching himself on an ornate chair in front of the bay windows of his vast house, I notice his blazer, cufflinks and belt all display his famous 'DG' insignia.

"You can supply, and I'll run it"

The splendour that surrounds us is a far cry from Gold's harrowing upbringing in the desperate years spanning World War II. Growing up in the poverty-mired East End of London, his first taste of business was a subsistence enterprise helping his mother sell bits and pieces from a stall at their home.

But going without in a post-war world was only one of many obstacles for the young Gold: his father was a petty criminal and philanderer, bullies picked on him at school for being Jewish and most horrific of all he was subjected to sexual abuse by his step-uncle.

In his adolescent years he found work as an apprentice bricklayer, a job that he detested, and Gold soon became sensitive to new career opportunities. When one came along he grabbed it without much consideration: "My brother was a book and magazine rep and he was selling to the guy that was running this bookstore," says Gold in-between sips of tea.

"The shop owner got into financial problems and couldn't pay my brother's bill or the landlord's. They were crying on each other's shoulders because their customer had gone bust. Then my brother tells me the story and I said, 'Why don't we take the shop over? You can supply it and I'll run it'."

"Getting investment is horrible"

Gold developed an aptitude for buying and selling through his family business, which though it was meagre and the end-game was survival, not profit, it ran on the same basic business principles (buy low, sell high) as the biggest and most profitable city-based firms.

An early hurdle was the £150 in back-rent the landlord demanded in exchange for his keys to the business. Neither David nor his brother had the money and Gold resorted to pitching to banks for a loan. It was the start of a long learning curve for the young entrepreneur.

"Getting investment is horrible. Every time you go, being rejected, it's like having a girlfriend saying she doesn't want to go out with you any more. But the key to rejection is: what did you learn from it? You learn a little bit and then another little bit and eventually you go in and make such a good presentation because you won't make a single mistake."

Cash safely in hand, Gold got the business off to a disappointingly slow start. He cut out all distractions in his life, including his potentially lucrative skill with a football, and focused on the business, which although it was located in a side street enjoyed a prime Charing Cross location. A stroke of luck changed everything. He left the store open till 10pm, because his brother had broken down and couldn't pick him up.

"This was winter time, and people on the main street walking in the darkness could see the little lights in my window and the displays. In those extra few hours we sold more stock than we had done all week. The following day I did the same thing and sure enough the same thing happened."

Filth and football

Noticing that stories with a sex theme sold well, he separated the naughtier books and upped his prices. As trade continued apace he began publishing his own books (like a supermarket stocking own brand food) and gradually bolted on complimentary businesses, including a distribution firm and a print works.

His success in publishing put him on the radar of porn magnate David Sullivan. Instead of competing they joined forces, Gold buying into Sullivan's *Sport* newspaper group – responsible for headlines such as 'World War II Bomber Found on the Moon' and 'Neil Kinnock's Grandparents Were Homosexual Martians' – and selling his stake in 2007.

Gold and Sullivan also shared a passion for football and the pair bought Birmingham City Football Club from administration in 1993 for a reported £700,000. Soon after the club was relegated to the then-second division, but enjoyed better fortunes in ensuing years. The club listed on AIM and with Karen Brady – the Premier League's only female chief executive – in charge the business made a £4.3m profit in 2008.

Gold and Sullivan sold their shares in Birmingham City to Hong Kong-based businessman Carson Yeung in 2009. In 2010 they bought a 50% stake in West Ham United, the childhood local team of Gold.

Ann Summers

Apart from a selection of other business interest which came and went over the years – a private air ferrying here, a lingerie shop there – Gold's main source of income since the seventies has been Ann Summers, the legendary purveyor of titillations he bought as a chain of just two stores in 1972.

Like in the case of his bookshop, Ann Summers built up gradually until a change of tack rocketed it into the realms of high street iconography. By the 1980s Gold had built his chain to seven shops, catering in those days to a male-orientated market and suffering from a seedy image.

Meanwhile, his daughter Jacqueline was heading up a new direct sales network called Party Plan. It brought together an all-female sales team who would arrange parties at customers' houses and sell them and their friends adult games, toys and garments over a few glasses of wine.

So popular was the service – it employed 7,000 sales women in its fourth year – that Gold was persuaded to emulate the idea in his bricks and mortar shops. Selecting his flagship store on London's Charing Cross Road for the experiment, because it needed refurbishing anyway, he put the wheels in motion.

It has now spread to 150 shops in the UK (20 more planned) and although sales have been up and down in recent years they averaged £122m between 2002 and 2008.

WAYNE HEMINGWAY MBE

Scourge of Fashionistas and Identikit Builders

Red or Dead co-founder Wayne Hemingway made his name on the catwalks of London, New York and Paris as a politically-driven fashion mogul. Having grown tired of the "shallow" industry and selling up, he is now on a mission to rid the world of bad design.

Hemingway HQ

Hemingway Design is the name given to a loose cluster of architectural, design and innovation projects led by the Hemingway family and orchestrated by Red or Dead co-founders Wayne and Gerardine, who lend their surname to the business. Its headquarters are domiciled in an unimposing semi-detached house halfway up a leafy suburban road in Wembley, north London.

That may seem a peculiar address from which to coordinate a cutting-edge business, but according to Wayne there's no need for a swanky centrally-located office. The Hemingways spend much of their time working on projects outside the capital and the remarkable story of Red or Dead means its founders don't need an impressive command centre to prove their credentials.

Inside, it looks as if a physical merger is taking place between an art studio and someone's home. There are telltale signs of domesticity, including a family kitchen leading to a generously proportioned garden, but everywhere are traces of the house's role as a place of work. (Including multi-coloured office furniture.)

Wayne intercepts me in the hallway. He is slim, bald and looks a lot younger than his 48 years. He wears a shirt, jeans and a pair of trademark designer spectacles. We shake hands and he welcomes me in, but I sense he isn't wholly at ease with a journalist in the house.

Some entrepreneurs, especially those who have sold a business for a lot of money, enjoy settling into an interview and talking at length. But Hemingway talks sparingly, getting to the point with the minimum of puff.

Any canvas, anywhere

Today, Hemingway presides over a mass of projects encompassing commercial, philanthropic and political spheres. An outspoken critique of 'affordable' housing he is on the board of numerous public committees and forums, does some charity work and is a regular speaker on the subjects of housing, urban design and education. All of which has earned him a string of honorary doctorates and professorships as well as an MBE from the Queen.

Income-earning projects include the renovation of the Institute of Directors' club on Pall Mall in London, a line of practical garden sheds, 'Roadrunner' retro fold-up bikes and a housing development of 3000 new homes in Lothian, Scotland. The canvas itself isn't important; if design is involved, then the Hemingways are interested.

Paradoxically, Wayne's propensity to attack publicly what he sees as "crap design" has landed him more than one juicy contract in the past. His biggest challenge to date is a commission to help plan, design and landscape an 800-property housing project on Tyneside for Taylor Wimpey homes. That came as a response to him speaking out against the "Wimpeyfication" of Britain and the spread of "identikit rabbit hutches".

"Quite often projects come to us because of my media profile," says Hemingway earnestly. "I might make a statement about something being terrible or ugly and sometimes the builder or owner agrees. We never advertised and never used a PR company, but we're in a pretty unique position because people in the industry have respect for the things we have done."

Having Wayne Hemingway on your books is a double-edged sword, though, especially if he sees you as responsible for the uglification of Britain. Taylor Wimpey received gushing admiration and extra column inches in the press for its collaboration with Hemingway Design, but the price was their new team-mate's constant belligerence.

"It's the work I'm most proud of since selling Red or Dead," he says with a wave of the hand. "Imagine how tough it is to change a national house builder like Wimpey and get them to create something that frightened them half to death. The project is hugely profitable and successful yet both sides were ready to pull out on more than one occasion."

At least recessions make you think

The Hemingways have enjoyed successes in other projects too. Even with the UK clawing its way out of recession the business is holding up, its growth hedged by the variety of projects on its books which insulate from a downturn led by retail, financial services and house prices. Wayne goes so far as suggesting he "likes" recessions because "they make you think". In his case, the thought process led to a new line of shed offices, which help people to work from home.

But he also thinks they improve the economy by removing obsolete industries and finishing off bad businesses: "I'm happy that Woolworths closed down, because it didn't serve the public selling pick 'n' mix. It's great that the car industry is suffering too because why should people need a new car every three years?

"This is a housing-led recession which makes homes more affordable and it has brought down the cost of mortgages. It's sad that people have to lose jobs and that there is short-term pain, but they'll end up working to create things that the world actually needs."

It is just as well Hemingway enjoys a good downturn. It was after a particularly nasty one that Wayne and his then-girlfriend (now wife)

Gerardine founded the business that was to make their name. In 1982, with the UK only just getting over double-digit interest rates, sky-high inflation, plus three million people unemployed, the pair started selling second-hand clothing from stalls on Kensington and Camden markets.

From markets to M&S

Initially, the young Hemingways sifted through car-boot sales and their own wardrobes for stock to sell, but the business took off when Gerardine started designing her own fashion lines. According to legend, Red or Dead's first big order came from Macy's in New York soon after the business set up shop and the contract was delivered from a small, hastily-opened manufacturing unit in Blackburn.

"We didn't need much money when we started," says Hemingway with a casual air. There was a fashion for vintage clothes so we took a few 10 pence pieces to jumble sales and bought as much stuff as we could. We started to make money early on so we never needed funding and never struggled."

"As the business developed we needed a bit more money to buy fabric, but the costs stayed low. In those days a stall in Camden market cost £6 a day, in Kensington market it was £12 a week. Our first big shop on Neal Street in Covent Garden cost £60 a week – it's more like £4000 now."

Shops were kitted out in vintage fittings and displays made from second-hand items – a popular look that the Hemingways pioneered. Today big retail players still sell marked-up second-hand items, but they pay shopfitters a premium to create the same 'shabby chic' effect.

From there, Red or Dead developed into a global business with 15 shops and hundreds of concessions all over the world. The head office grew to 100 designers and creative staff, and the Hemingways started making ripples in the fashion industry.

Initially horrified by the company's approach – Wayne and Gerardine shunned the normal parties, freebies and celebrity endorsements – the fashionistas gradually accepted Red or Dead as a major player and it started picking up big contracts with established shop chains (including M&S) and a string of awards followed.

"The success and growth of Red or Dead didn't surprise us," Hemingway remembers. "We were just kids then and I don't think we were really old enough to realise that what was happening was unusual. We just thought that was how it happens."

And the secret of Hemingway's success? "We didn't make a lot of mistakes so we were able to grow quickly. More importantly we weren't afraid to fail so we never wrote a business plan and we never planned or strategised a lot. As long as you are close enough to your business you should know when something is going wrong and be brave enough to just stop it."

Jennifer Irvine

Feeder to the Stars

Jennifer Irvine is a young mother of three and an entrepreneur with a thriving food delivery business. She takes both roles very seriously, but ask her which is harder and it's mother every time. Going to work "is like taking a break" for this multi-tasking businesswoman.

Emotional chef syndrome

When Jennifer Irvine founded The Pure Package, a service providing clients with three balanced meals a day created with their sex, shape and 'health goals' in mind, she had two things weighing against her: her age (27) and her gender (female).

Now with her business' sales topping £1m a year and a constellation of celebrity customers including model Erin O'Connor, actor Hugh Jackman and TV star Patsy Kensit on her books, Irvine has surmounted these obstacles emphatically – and on the odd occasion has used them to her advantage.

But in the early days the blonde-haired, blue-eyed, attractive Irvine struggled to convince others she was the real deal. Upon setting up her kitchen, obtaining the necessary licences and acquiring a small customer base her first chef promptly abandoned her, complaining that he didn't think she was serious about the business.

"My first chef thought I was pursuing a hobby. There are things you can't change and there's no point in dwelling on the negative. Sometimes it's a little bit frustrating when an electrician comes in and they insist on speaking to the kitchen porter because he's a man and you're a woman. But I wouldn't change it; I wouldn't like to have to shave every day," she chuckles.

Pure profits

Structural growth is fuelled by profits and nothing else.

She is the owner of the firm and as such looks after its accounts (a simple task as long as you can add and subtract, she says), strategic direction and PR, but the sourcing, cooking and delivery are orchestrated by staff at The Pure Package's New Covent Garden Market headquarters in Vauxhall, South London.

The business thrives on word of mouth and before the recession of 2008-9 growth was blazing at 40% or 50% per year. Irvine has cut its marketing budget to let the buzz take care of itself. Partly as a result, celebrity clientele have replaced wealthy City workers as the business' main source of growth.

"Most of our clients come from referrals, so that is always going to keep things strong. Celeb-wise there'll be a big get-together – like Elton John's birthday or something like that, and there'll be an influx of celebrities because they'll all see each other and say 'Oh you look gorgeous', 'No you look gorgeous' – and when everybody gets to hear about The Pure Package, the whole table will come to us."

"A walk-in chiller in my garden"

Another reason for The Pure Package's growth is its structure. Irvine started up in her own ten-by-six foot kitchen which was capable of feeing just nine customers. She already had the essential components of her business: a freezer, oven and a computer, so capital outlay was minimal in the beginning.

Irvine picked up her first clients by writing to food critics and inviting them to go on a plan free of charge, and in return answer a survey about the service. Some of the journalists opted to cover the new business in newspapers and magazines (though Irvine hadn't asked for this) and soon she had her nine paying customers.

"Within a few days of launch I was at capacity and then I had to get a new fridge-freezer in the spare bedroom and then a walk-in chiller in my back garden – and then within a month or so I had to move the business out of my house. It was crazy," she reflects.

With low overheads and clients paying in advance, cash flow and profits were easy to schedule and Irvine plotted a course for business growth with a lot more certainty than the average fledgling entrepreneur.

Referrals – the best marketing there is – underpin trust in the brand, as do the awards Irvine has won over the years. They include Shell LiveWIRE Young Entrepreneur of the Year in 2005, BT Essence of an Entrepreneur in 2006 and Harper's Bazaar Entrepreneur of the Year in 2007.

"When you win an award from a big organisation it validates your brand. Now I've got people buying 90 days' food in advance. Recently someone bought food for himself, his wife, his PA, his hairdresser, the whole entourage and paid for five months' food up front – that's £10,000 to £20,000."

Convenience and nutrition

The service itself is all about convenience and nutrition. It's targeted at the wealthy – prices start at £150 a week and the top packages are double that – and busy people who care about the food they eat or want to achieve some sort of goal: losing weight or building up energy reserves, for example.

A busy mother of three, Irvine is a customer as well the proprietor ("I get my food delivered every day from The Pure Package. It's lovely, couldn't do without it," she says). It's good to hear she puts her mouth where her money is, so to speak.

"Fad diets are on the whole terrible," says Irvine explaining why The Pure Package is preferable. "We're all about perfectly balanced diets." Nutritional specialists meet with new customers and ensure "the correct number of fruit and vegetables a day, essential fats and so on. We get a lot of clients referred to us from trainers, nutritional therapists or doctors."

It's a sensible approach that has investors banging down her door, but although Irvine won't rule out bringing in the money men, she is adamant that financiers must reflect the pious aims of the business.

"I would consider taking on investment and giving away equity in my business, because I think the business has so much opportunity still," she says, but adds that investors might be put off by her valuation. "I don't know if people would be that interested in getting involved because I think the business is so valuable."

It may mean that The Pure Package continues its organic – and it should be said still impressive – growth pattern without involvement from men in pinstripe suits. That's not a problem for its founder who is enjoying the experience of being a successful mother.

Mumpreneurs

I ask what would be her advice to other mothers who harbour entrepreneurial ambitions. "I think that maternity leave could be a really great opportunity for somebody to start a business," she replies. "It can be a wonderful opportunity, especially after your first child.

"When your life gets jigged around you're able to recognise some opportunities that you wouldn't recognise normally. You might think there's a huge market of mothers and nobody has invented x, y or z. It's a huge chance to suddenly have these new ideas."

So enthusiastic is she about the combination of business and motherhood that Irvine is planning more kids in the future. "I need a break though," she admits. "I've been pregnant or breast-feeding for four years and I could do with my body back for a bit!"

PETER JONES CBE

The Dragon Who Doesn't Breathe Fire

Peter Jones is involved with 30 businesses, a fistful of adverts, a string of TV shows and even has time for a philanthropic streak with his very own enterprise academy. Oh and he has five kids too. But this frenetic entrepreneur just can't get enough.

Head-banging tycoon

"I'm glad I'm tall," says Peter Jones, the six-foot seven-inch founder of Phones International Group, business angel and latterly TV personality. "It definitely has its advantages in business when you need to have a presence. I'd stop short of using the word imposing though. The flipside is you can look a bit of a prat when the first thing you do when you walk into a meeting is bang your head!"

Jones is a gentle giant despite what you might hear, read or watch (in case you haven't noticed, he's a regular in the media). He is softly spoken and if he makes a point he'll mitigate it with phrases like "perhaps" or "a little bit". It's a contrast to the fiery image he portrays on *Dragons' Den*, the phenomenally popular BBC series which made his name with the viewing public. The same could be said of fellow dragon Deborah Meaden, though not James Caan who talks quietly anyway.

"*Dragons' Den* happened completely out of the blue. I'm still surprised that the public seem to love watching me on television," he jokes. "It certainly opens doors in business, because people want to meet me or become involved in one of my portfolio businesses a lot more than they did before I became famous." He has also appeared in *American Inventor* and *Tycoon*, similar business-themed programmes.

Backing the worthwhile

Jones protests that his TV appearances hope to inspire others to make a fortune like his own, estimated at about £160m. Indeed, he is one of Britain's most prominent mavens of entrepreneurship and takes every opportunity to sing its praises. He fronts BT's Essence of the Entrepreneur scheme and has ploughed £3m of his own money into a National Enterprise Academy, which over the next three years will train 30,000 wannabe Peter Joneses. He also advertised Moneysupermarket.com, the price comparison website started by fellow multi-millionaire Simon Nixon.

"I don't do adverts for the money; in fact I donate the proceeds. I just think it's important to back organisations that do something worthwhile. BT is getting behind fledgling entrepreneurs and helping them succeed. Moneysupermarket.com helps people save money – what could be better at a time like this?"

Jones claims he agreed to front an ad campaign for the website after he himself saved money on car insurance. "It might sound really strange to you, but just because you have cash doesn't mean you don't care about cutting costs," he laughs.

There is sense in his words though. Our interview coincides with almost the worst recession in living memory. Jones describes the situation as "tough" but declares himself an optimist and says the recovery is already underway: "It will be like a Nike tick," he muses. "Not a dramatic rise but a steady return to growth."

Feedback not failure

He reckons more people should think like him, and in entrepreneurial terms it's hard not to agree. Jones is driven but not aggressive and positive without being daft. He also has great sympathy for those who fail in business; in fact he wants the word 'failure' removed from the English language.

This sentiment is not born from some moral high ground but bitter experience. He lost everything with his first attempts in business and had to start again with Phones International in 1998. Working and (though his staff didn't know it) sleeping in a small office, Jones built the company into a business with annual sales hitting £150m.

"There is no such word as failure to me. I wasn't great at school and it was crushing when I tried my best and a teacher turned around and said 'you failed'. It's really just feedback. You learn from your mistakes and good entrepreneurs will use that knowledge on their next venture."

"I thought it would go on forever"

He started acting like a businessman at age 12, before knowing what the word entrepreneur meant. At 16 he created a tennis academy and by his early twenties was at the helm of his own computer company, which provided him with a brief taste of millionairedom.

"I had a nice house and a couple of cars and all the spare money I needed to have a good time," Jones remembers. "I thought it was fantastic and that it would go on forever, but I made a few careless errors, a few clients went bust and my business soon went under."

After starting and losing another computer business and a restaurant, a "flat broke", homeless and carless Jones was forced back into the world of employment with a large corporate business. He soon shone in his new role and before long took control of a country division.

But the entrepreneurial calling nagged at him and Jones founded Phones International Group aged 32, just four years later. It quickly achieved huge success with £14m in first-year sales, climbing at an astounding rate to £44m in the second year. The business hit a growing market and expanded with the uptake of mobile communications. It provides phone handsets and accessories to retailers, as well as telecoms-infrastructure services to businesses. With new companies sprouting up within the group all the time, it is still responsible for the vast majority of Jones' wealth.

Den additions

But with every series of *Dragons' Den*, he adds new interests and new opportunities to make money. Since 2008, the economic downturn has given the game show a fresh appeal as the Dragons search for recession-proof ideas and rugged entrepreneurs able to push their ideas to the top.

No more crazy punts like Rachel Elnaugh's Le Beanock swinging beanbags or Simon Woodroffe's investment in a youth who wanted to start a truffle farm in France. So far Jones' runaway success in the Den has been Reggae Reggae Sauce, fronted by Levi Roots who quickly became a successful entrepreneur in his own right.

Like its ubiquitous owners, the Caribbean-inspired condiment is all over the place. Straightaway Jones was able to get it into the biggest supermarket chains and a subsequent joint venture with Subway has taken the brand into the stratosphere with a big advertising campaign.

"Levi Roots deserves a lot of credit, it's an incredible story and he achieved success in no time. He is a very, very special guy and I'm glad I came into contact with him to give him the chance he needed," beams Jones.

But Jones concedes that it isn't just about the warm, gooey feeling he gets from making someone else a millionaire. "To be blunt it's good for my bank balance as well, the business makes an absolute fortune."

KANYA KING MBE

The Woman Who Brought Recognition to Black Music

Having struggled initially to get off the ground, the MOBO Awards (Music of Black Origin) have become a globally recognised brand attracting some of the world's biggest stars to Britain every year. Its founder, Kanya King, is philosophical about her triumph and refuses to capitalise commercially if it means endangering the show's founding principles.

From no budget to 250 million viewers

When Kanya King set up the MOBO Awards in 1996, she had no event-organising experience, no budget and no time. Yet the show she put on won over a national TV network and drew celebrities including Lennox Lewis, Lionel Richie and, erm, Tony Blair.

That first hastily constructed show at London's New Connaught Rooms also kicked off a legacy that has not only endured but snowballed in the years since. The autumn 2009 event, held in Glasgow's SECC – the first to take place outside London – was viewed by 250 million people on TV sets across the world.

R&B sensation Rihanna opened the show; champion boxer Amir Khan presented an award; and Beyoncé Knowles, who couldn't make it on the night, nevertheless took time out of a busy schedule to record a video message to her fans.

All this is not bad going for a university drop-out from the rough end of London.

"There was always the worry of the bills coming in"

King's parents were both first-generation immigrants to the UK, her father Ghanaian, her mother Irish: "This was still at a time when there were signs saying 'No blacks, no Irish, no dogs', but we couldn't afford a dog so that was something," she laughs.

Her upbringing was, needless to say, difficult; and it was made harder when her father died while King was still a child. The youngest girl of nine children, she shared a bedroom with four siblings while her mother worked a series of jobs just to keep a roof over their heads.

"My mother relied on me a lot and I got a lot of joy out of being able to prevent the gas or electricity being cut off," she says with happy intonations, as if the memory is nostalgic not painful. "There was always the worry of the bills coming in. She would ask, 'Kanya, what are we going to do?'

"So I was working from a young age and I was able to buy my own nice clothes. My mother had to go to jumble sales and of course vintage clothes are very fashionable now but we didn't think so at the time. I made sacrifices very early on and prioritised. That I suppose gave me the foundation to budget."

King had a paper round from the age of eight and among her early entrepreneurial schemes sold whistles at the Notting Hill Carnival for £1 each, having bought the instruments for 35p. Eventually her knack for making money meant she could leave the crowded family home and buy a place of her own.

A few career moves later, including – bizarrely – becoming a founding member of the production team on TV's short-lived Chrystal Rose show, King was ready to go into business. So confident was she of her idea about an awards ceremony celebrating black music that her first move was to remortgage the house.

She launched the MOBO Organisation from her bedroom and became the embodiment of the 'fake it till you make it' school of business. "I was surrounded by my laundry and people would ring up and I'd say proudly 'The MOBO Organisation, can I help?' – they didn't need to know where I was operating from."

"It worked because I had passion. The music was selling massive amounts, but there was no platform on which the artists that performed in these genres could celebrate their talent. That's why I was happy to work so hard to get it up and running."

"Everything had to be perfect"

King's big break was a chance encounter at a football stadium with the then-head of LWT. He was looking for his son and while coming to his aid she took a gamble and told him of her plans for MOBO. A few weeks later she was at Carlton Television headquarters finalising broadcasting rights for the launch event.

Immediate problems included lack of budget and a tiny six-week window to prepare the show. Having grabbed the opportunity, King began to wonder if it was possible after all. At least getting the artists wasn't a problem, they had nowhere else to showcase their music on such a prestigious stage.

"What made me think that I could succeed where other people failed was that I was able to think long-term," she reminisces with a determined air. "Some people tried to do it as a way to make a quick buck. I knew that we wouldn't have the resources for the fireworks and the dancers and everything else.

"But I felt that we could make it glamorous by encouraging people to dress up and we had a salubrious location; all the ingredients you need to make a show-stopper. Everything from the look of the invite onwards had to be perfect. I was prepared to invest in it personally too and I think that had a lot to do with it working."

Nearly 15 years on King treats each new event with the same gusto. Her soft tones and kindly nature belie a determined streak that is a vital ingredient in cracking the music industry; be you an artist, manager or glitzy event organiser.

The events do the talking

King has come a long way from her bedroom office in the mid-nineties, but she sees no need for grand, glass-fronted headquarters.

A 'statement' office would be a waste of money, she argues. The events speak for themselves. Besides, nowadays suppliers are falling over themselves to team up with the MOBO brand and King outsources just about every task that isn't absolutely necessary to be performed in-house. Only a handful of staff are employed full-time. "When you start up in business – and we are all guilty of this – you try to do everything yourself and then when you grow you recruit staff to take over all the roles. But now we outsource as much as possible and it has completely changed our strategic view. Now we work with experts and even though some freelancers are practically full-time here it means they can focus on one job and do it perfectly."

MOBO works with many of the same people every year, but critical parts of the formula, such as set design, always go out to tender. Sitting next to me on the table is a scale mock-up model sent in by one hopeful design agency. "We're not using that one," she smiles.

In many ways MOBO is not like any other business featured in this book. Revenues are still heavily dependent on its annual flagship event, meaning that sales spike once a year. King is not as profit-hungry as other entrepreneurs and admits commercial opportunities thrown up by the MOBO brand are yet to be explored.

King herself is not a millionaire, though she could be many times over if she wanted. She reserves only a small amount of MOBO's proceeds for herself, and other proceeds are reinvested in the business or spent on charity work.

MARTHA LANE FOX

Dotcom Survivor

Still in her mid-30s Martha Lane Fox has experienced more than her fair share of agony and ecstasy. Nearly six years after the accident that should have killed her, she remains in recovery. But disobeying her battered body, the Lastminute.com entrepreneur has found the strength to rekindle her business career.

"It reconfirmed to me the things that were really important"

A single moment on 2 May 2004 caused Martha Lane Fox's world to collapse. In a swerve of a car on a wet Moroccan road, she went from triumphant dotcom entrepreneur to a broken roadside casualty with years of rehabilitation and therapy ahead of her.

Lane Fox was taking a well-earned break only months after stepping down as group managing director of Lastminute.com. She had amassed a £5m fortune through her successful development of the online brand and could expect at least three times that amount from shares she retained in the business.

Driving with friends in an open-top jeep, she opted not to buckle her seat belt for the short trip between the restaurant where they lunched and the beach which was the destination for the afternoon. So when the car skidded on a puddle, she was thrown clean from the passenger seat – landing on an exposed desert rock.

Before the accident, the only way was up for Lane Fox: "I was offered the job to run Selfridges. I didn't start, I didn't get there. I had the accident two weeks before I was due to start. I spent two years in and out of hospital. I got through it with a lot of drugs – a lot of morphine and a lot of help," she explains.

"You have to change irrevocably when you've had to learn everything again, from walking to thinking. I think it reconfirmed to me the things that were really important to me like my family and friends."

Champion, chairman and more

Lane Fox has just accepted an offer to become Britain's first 'Digital Inclusion Champion', an unpaid government post within the Department for Communities, responsible for improving Britain's socioeconomic troubles through the internet and technology as a whole.

No small task. Although her official job spec is a bit vague, Lane Fox is excited by the challenge: "It is early days and we've hit the ground running, as they say. It's far too interesting and complex a subject to miss out on and I hope I can bring some interesting ideas to the problem," she says with customary modesty.

The role is a full-time job in itself, but Lane Fox has to juggle it with a suite of other commitments. She is founder and chairman of karaoke bar chain Lucky Voice and a non-executive director of Marks & Spencer, Channel 4 and mydeco.com – a furniture shop where you can design your rooms online.

She founded Antigone, a grant-giving foundation that supports start-up charities in the fields of criminal justice, health and education. She even finds time to be a trustee of Reprieve, a charity looking after the rights of prisoners. Despite her millions, Lane Fox is a bit of a lefty and a great believer in social justice; she once upon a time dreamt of becoming a prison governor, not a dotcom magnate.

She's busy all right, but at least life is never dull: "The only thing that is consistent about my days is that they start at six o'clock in the morning because I don't sleep very well. I power through my emails early, do a lot of exercise and go through my physio for the day.

"Then I'll go to one of four or five places, depending on what's happening that day. I'm peripatetic, but my main challenge of the day is trying to grapple with all these different issues from different businesses, trying to find the commonality amongst them and link up different bits of them."

"We were incredibly mean"

It all started in 1998 when, together with colleague Brent Hoberman, Lane Fox founded Lastminute.com, a website advertising late-breaking deals in travel and leisure which came to epitomise the tumultuous dotcom boom period. In this era most dotcoms followed a similar pattern: founded on a flimsy business plan, they raised vast amounts of investment capital on the promise of swift returns and multiples in the hundreds. Then, after a period of unchecked spending, they ran out of money and shrivelled like balloons.

In stark contrast, Lastminute.com initially raised just £600,000. At the time it was the biggest amount handed to a British internet start-up, but it paled into insignificance compared with the amounts bandied around in the years that followed.

"We thought we had taken on more money than we could possibly imagine," says Lane Fox innocently. "Things rapidly changed in the build up to 2000 with multi-million pound deals being done, but we thought it was a hell of a lot of money and we managed our cash very carefully. We were incredibly mean."

Apart from being frugal with the cash, the business flourished in the dotcom boom because it rested on sound business principles. The technology, products and service delivery were all in line with customer expectations, while the PR lavished on the buccaneering young entrepreneurs was unprecedented in the internet world.

It all added up to a monster success. But even with a sound business plan, Lastminute.com never completely escaped the clutches of boom hysteria until it was well and truly over. After listing on the stock market the site's share price soared to 487p, valuing it a whisker under three-quarters of a billion pounds.

Over the next 18 months it collapsed down to £32m as the boom turned to bust and reality set in for hitherto excitable investors. But when Martha quit the company in December 2003 it had once again climbed – this time definitely on the strength of the business – to £667m.

"It's much worse to leave a business when it's not going well and I wanted to bow out when it was going brilliantly. I always said I would leave when we reached profitability and that's what I did," she says.

"It wasn't a surprise to Brent, I loved it dearly but it's the mark of a good business if it's not reliant on any one person, be that me or Brent or anyone else. So I felt proud that I could walk out of the door and it would have no real impact on the business at all."

Rubber Chicken

It was while holidaying in Tokyo early in 2004 that Lane Fox stumbled on the idea for Lucky Voice, her new venture. "It's a complete copycat. I'm like a magpie stealing other people's ideas. Some friends and I went to Japan and we did a 24-hour sing in Tokyo, we didn't sing the same song twice. It was quite extraordinary."

The point of Lucky Voice is not to preen and display like an X Factor contestant, but to enjoy the experience of singing in a group, according to Lane Fox. "We're not trying to do it in a hip or trendy way, just to make it fun. There's no performing, but you have cocktails and food and have a sing – that's it."

After a measured start, hampered in part by the hospitalisation of the chairman, managing director Nick Thistleton has grown the business quickly in the last two years. There are five venues sprinkled across London, Manchester, Cardiff and Brighton, as well as concessions in partner bars and a growing online platform offering streamed karaoke classics to sing along to at home.

The name itself derives from a survey of Japanese office workers. Asked what they would call a new karaoke bar the top answer came out as

Lucky Voice, preferred by the founders to 'Rubber Chicken'. "To this day I don't know why they came back with that," Lane Fox chuckles.

STEVE LEACH

The Internet's Very Own Big Mouth

In a meandering 20-year career Steve Leach has sold oversized ladies lingerie, worked as a fireman and a commercial pilot – and founded £160m turnover Bigmouthmedia, Europe's largest independent digital marketing agency. Now having sold half his business, the Edinburgh-based entrepreneur is looking for more growth and new challenges.

4,111% growth

According to the Deloitte 'Technology Fast 50', Bigmouthmedia was one of the top ten fastest growing British-based technology companies in 2009. Recording a growth rate of 4,111% in the previous five years, the business has swelled because of soaring demand for online marketing and by merging with or acquiring its competitors.

Pay-per-click (PPC), search engine optimisation (SEO), social media and online display are all multi-billion dollar industries, having risen with the development of internet services in the last 15 years. Big Mouth, founded in 1997, mastered each of these online advertising vehicles as it emerged, incorporating them into the company armoury and selling them to the world's biggest brands.

Companies like Tesco, Adidas, British Airways, Top Man, Samsung and Starbucks have all benefited from a bigger presence on the internet thanks to Bigmouth. So big is the client portfolio that Bigmouth's budget for Google AdWords alone runs into hundreds of millions of pounds.

The man heading up this pioneering enterprise is Steve Leach, a Scottish entrepreneur whose background gives few hints of his aptitude for new media.

Bigbrand

The last time I met him was when he won an 'entrepreneur of the year' gong at the Growing Business Awards. Leach has grown to enjoy his awards 'dos' and has become something of a collector in recent times. In consecutive years he won a hat trick of top entrepreneurial accolades in Scotland, Britain and, in 2008, Europe, while also pocketing industry gongs for Bigmouth's many excellent achievements in the digital media world.

"Business awards have certainly helped to push us where we are today," he says with a contented smile. "They can be overlooked by business leaders but people want to work for best-of breeds and industry awards improve your reputation in the market, so I think they're worth their weight in gold."

Entrepreneur judges applaud his steering of the good ship Bigmouthmedia through the capricious winds of the early internet era when would-be customers were sceptical of its benefits and doubted the huge four- and five-figure percentage returns on investment that tools like pay-per-click professed to offer.

They congratulate Leach and his co-founder-cum-marketing director wife Heather on their skilful development of the brand and for Steve's dogged unwillingness to sell equity in the business until the right offer came along. When he did sell a stake, towards the end of 2006, it was part of a complicated reverse takeover with a German rival which put him in the driving seat of the enlarged business.

The Scottish *Sunday Times*' Rich List says the Leach family's earnings from the deal coupled with their retained stake in Bigmouth earned them an £80m fortune, just £5m shy of Sean Connery a couple of places above them on the list.

Carlyle Group, which originated the deal and made the investment, concluded that Bigmouthmedia had the stronger of the two brands despite being much smaller than Global Media, the German business it reversed into. The merged entity took on the Bigmouth identity, driving the brand into the realm of new media royalty.

"For years we held off selling," says Leach after taking a sip of beer and reclining into his chair. "My wife and I owned 90% of the business and we were making multi-million profits so what we had was very valuable. That's where my hair went: turning down offers in the double-digit millions to buy the business.

"We were living in a normal semi-detached house and had an average car, so turning down that much money was really hard and to be honest it nearly broke me. We eventually accepted the offer we couldn't refuse from Carlyle, which gave us much more money than the other offers and we retained a 40% stake in the business."

"It's definitely time to consolidate"

With the stress of fast growth, mergers and new investors to contend with, Leach is pleased that the recession happened when it did. It took pressure off what was becoming unsustainable growth. In 2009-10 Leach expected a double-digit increase in sales – a snail's pace next to the previous five years.

He is taking stock, cutting back on unnecessary expenditure, lowering staff numbers in some areas and increasing them in others, automating certain practices, hedging Bigmouth's exposure to foreign-exchange fluctuations, paying off debts and in general making the business fitter and more efficient.

But the downturn is also giving the cash-rich Bigmouthmedia opportunities to do some business on the cheap. Whereas before the downturn good media businesses were being valued at 15 times their annual profits, now he can acquire firms for much lower multiples.

"It's definitely time to consolidate and make some acquisitions. Before, the multiples meant you wouldn't see your money again for six or seven years; now we're looking at one or two. We're making a few smallish purchases but something big could come along soon," he says cautiously.

The accidental internet tycoon

Leach himself fell into the internet marketing game almost by accident. Having built up and sold a women's lingerie business with his partner Heather at the age of just 21, Leach spent a few years as a fireman and then nine months as a commercial pilot ("It wasn't even anywhere near as good as being a taxi driver," he moans).

In 1994, Leach asked a friend to build him a computer and, having become interested in the process decided to start a business installing PCs and networks for corporate clients. By 1996, in lightning quick time, a now Microsoft-qualified Leach was running one of the biggest computer network installation firms in Scotland, with profits in the hundreds of thousands. His firm was riding the rush of businesses suddenly gripped by the urge to computerise and get networked.

Having merged his business with his hardware supplier Leach "got a bit bored to be honest" and sold his stake to his business partner, exiting completely. He correctly identified that the market would slow down and that the internet was the new Wild West.

"I thought there was definitely something in the internet," he grins "and I also noticed the consolidation in the hardware market – brands were absorbing each other. I thought we had a limited window so I sold my share to my partner and I set up Bigmouth." Starting life as a basic online marketing firm Bigmouthmedia began picking up clients and gradually moved into areas such as pay-per-click and social media as they emerged. Bigmouthmedia now has over 200 staff in 13 global offices including a fleet of SEO (search engine optimisation) experts – genuine geeks, not just people with a loose grip on the technology.

SEO specialists

"I would say there are about 12 people in the UK who can genuinely claim to be real SEO experts," says Leach confidently. "Not just people who can make a difference but proper geek geniuses who like dark rooms and are at the top of their game. We have two of them, I'd say."

To prevent these über-geeks moving on, Leach has furnished them with shares in the business and a host of perks. Big companies are always on the lookout for such wonders and will pay salaries of up to £250,000 to get hold of them. Like most switched-on entrepreneurs will tell you, good people are critical to the goals of your business.

DEBORAH MEADEN

From Holiday Parks to *Dragons' Den*

*D*ragons' Den investor Deborah Meaden made millions growing and selling her family's holiday park business. She puts her triumph down to good judgement and sticking to basic business principles. She sees no reason why others can't follow suit.

Business and bloodlines

Deborah Meaden is coy about the story of her rise to entrepreneurial stardom. The first and only business she started, a glass and ceramics import outfit inspired by a trip to Florence, was a flop, and while she made a roaring success of the family firm she is reluctant to accept all the credit.

Leaving business school at 19 and running a medley of enterprises – from a fashion franchise to a prize bingo concession – with varying degrees of success, in 1988 Meaden went back on a vow to never join Weststar Holidays, the business set up by her mother and stepfather.

Starting on the lowest rung, overseeing slot machines, Meaden acquired a knack for business in the leisure sector and was quickly promoted to managing director of the firm. She revelled in the responsibility and transformed Weststar from a small family concern into a travel-industry notable with five locations in the west of England and 150,000 visitors per year.

"I don't want to be disrespectful to my parents because we had different goals, but the business looked very different when I sold the first chunk of it in 1999 to how it did when I joined a few years before," says Meaden, tiptoeing around the thorny issue of doing a better job than her mum.

Despite what she thinks, Meaden has every right to laud her success. For Weststar, the term 'family business' was a technicality and employees were denied preferential treatment because of bloodlines. The founders operated like any other business and she had to demonstrate merit before being rewarded with promotions.

When her parents exited the business and Meaden took over in a management buyout, the two sides of the transaction sought independent sets of advisers and in her own words negotiations became "pretty feisty" as the parties squabbled over price. Luckily the family mantra 'business is business' held firm and ties remained intact.

"At the time I paid a pretty full price for that business," she assures me. "I wanted to pay less; they wanted me to pay more, so we negotiated. That's how business works. In hindsight people might say it wasn't a lot of money, but I can tell you it was at the time," she adds, perhaps mindful of the killer profit she subsequently made.

Spooky timing

By 1999 the leisure market was the subject of growing interest from private equity firms and Weststar came under a barrage of cash offers. Having only recently bought the business Meaden was reluctant to sell straightaway, but her business brain reminded her that opportunities are there to be taken.

"I hadn't acquired the business to sell it so quickly, but the sector was hotting up. There were lots of people who wanted to enter the market and not many holiday parks around, so prices went northwards. The problem was if I waited until the timing was right for me, I could be selling just as the market hit rock bottom."

So Meaden agreed the happy medium of selling half her stake, 23% of the business, for £33m to Phoenix Equity Partners. She gradually loosened her grip on the leadership reigns, becoming investment director and a non-executive before exiting fully in 2007 and collecting a further £19m.

The two transactions gave Meaden a chance to exhibit her spookily good judgement and sense of timing. The 1999 equity sale was (and still might be) the most paid per pitch for a holiday park in the UK; meanwhile she estimates that her final exit eight years later was sealed two weeks before the first signs of the credit crunch appeared with Northern Rock's troubles.

Learning from the private equity pros

It was between sales of equity chunks in Weststar that Meaden developed a curiosity for the investment and investor-relations process – something that would lead into her replacing Rachel Elnaugh on the BBC's *Dragons' Den* in 2006. She says her experience with Phoenix was overwhelmingly positive and she applied lessons learned during the partnership to her new business interests.

"I take the same approach with my investees now. I feel like I've done the hard slog in business and I'm enjoying this gentle switch between being an operator and being the investor. I'm quite perceptive and I've got a good sense of what needs to be done in each business, which definitely helps the process."

All of the Dragons will tell you they want to partner with investors and not just frisk them for cash, but do they really mean it? Meaden certainly wants us to think she does, and for good reason: a happy entrepreneur is a profitable entrepreneur.

No negotiation

Her *Dragons' Den* style is distinct, though: careful consideration, followed (where it makes sense) by an offer – and then no negotiation whatsoever.

"I spend a lot of time sitting quietly, calculating my offer. Once I've made up my mind, the only way I would change it is if a new piece of information comes along. They might expect to negotiate, but that's not my style. I always make sure they're happy, though; the last thing I want to do is drag them in kicking and screaming!"

It's a system that has delivered some pretty impressive results. In series six Meaden co-invested with fellow Dragon Theo Paphitis in Magic Whiteboard, a polythene roll charged with static which sticks to surfaces without using adhesives. Both paid £50,000 for a 20% stake in the company. At the time it was turning over just £70,000; today, sales are hovering around the £1m mark.

Meaden is also excited about investments made outside the Den. She has just ploughed money into Fox Brothers, an ancient manufacturer of woollen and worsted cloth based in Somerset close to where she lives. The business was founded in 1640 and as such is a national business treasure, but in the last decade it has struggled to compete with newer firms.

"But the team is very motivated and they have a brilliant managing director, who I expect will eventually buy me out. The previous owner wanted to keep the business local, so it's perfect for me. I really like the business, which is so important too."

Products first

Unlike what many investors will tell you, Meaden readily admits she is far more interested in business itself than the team running it. The founders are, of course, extremely important, but forced to make the choice she would opt for a good product and a bad team over the reverse scenario.

"I employ good people, but when I'm looking for a business and not trying to recruit people I'm looking for the right product. It's a complete waste of a good person to spend all of their time on something that is fundamentally flawed.

"I think people get confused between employment and investing and if you invest in a good person with a bad product then basically all you're doing is paying a hefty recruitment fee, aren't you?"

By that rationale, Meaden would refuse an offer to invest in her own ceramics import business of 30 years ago. And with good reason: although she drew up contracts with customers guaranteeing they would buy only from her, retailers soon went to the manufacturers direct, and Meaden, having been cut out of the loop, was powerless to enforce the law.

The lesson here is: even if you have a suspicion you'll be worth £50m in future you had better create a pretty special business if you want to see any of Deborah Meaden's investment capital. It's a rule that she has learned the hard way.

ADRIAN MOORHOUSE

Going Swimmingly

Olympic gold-winning swimmer Adrian Moorhouse hasn't entered a pool since he retired from the sport in 1992 aged 28. Now he runs a human resources (HR) consultancy with annual sales topping £7m, yet, as he explains, his past remains ever-present. It's a blessing and a curse: the key thing is how he has learned not to be typecast or pigeonholed by where he's come from, but rather to adapt it to create a genuinely innovative and highly successful new business.

Laurels are not for resting upon, nor for abandoning

By and large, being the managing director of a £7m-turnover, 80-person business won't make you famous. Being a world-record-breaking Olympic gold medallist, on the other hand, will.

Like Botham, Thompson, Lineker, Torvill, Dean and Goodhew, the name Moorhouse is synonymous with British sporting prowess in the mid-to-late 1980s. His fame derives from a shock no-medal finish at the Atlanta Games in 1984 and reversing that disappointment by snatching gold at Seoul four years later.

His career was tumultuous to say the least; peppered with highs and lows beyond the spectrum of many sporting greats. An angst-ridden Moorhouse almost retired after the 'failure' of fourth place in '84, was stripped of gold at the World Championships two years later for an illegal turn (which wasn't) and won the finals at Seoul by a one-hundredth of a second.

After that any career choice would be a change of pace but not, as Moorhouse discovered, a change of profile. Having tried various coaching and sport committee roles he set up HR specialists Lane4 in

1995, yet even as the business picked up an impressive string of clients the 'ex-swimmer' tag followed him around.

"This is what I do now and it would be great to be recognised as 'that great businessman' and not 'that guy who used to swim'," says Moorhouse as we talk over coffee at a plush hotel on London's Strand. "For the first five years I banned PR and marketing and made it clear that if I got in the papers for sporting reasons there'd be a problem."

Moorhouse has retained his short hair and athletic build from his swimming days but shed the aggressive competitive streak that he admits used to alienate most of his fellow athletes. Now he is placid and softly spoken, delivering lengthy answers to my questions with a flattering level of concentration and care.

The fame issue, he believes, is a double-edged sword. For a start he probably would not appear in this book had he not been a famous swimmer. The same goes for speaking slots at major HR events and, though he hates to admit it, business opportunities too.

But this has just opened doors, and given him the opportunity to deliver his business learning and motivation to audiences and clients who are eager to listen. It is not the service itself. That and his related business success came from successfully adapting what he had learned from one world and applying it to another. "I want[ed] to create new ideas in the industry, not tell a story about how I used to swim."

The lessons of sport

Overall, Moorhouse reckons about 60% of what goes on in sport translates well to the business world. Even some things that don't have an obvious parallel can be very useful. Sporting ambition and athlete development tend to evolve in four-year cycles, for instance, in line with the occurrence of big competitions like the Olympics and football or rugby world cups. The same can't be said for business: but the goal-setting aspect of the four-year programme, with tangible future objectives (given realistic goal dates, neither too soon nor too delayed), is perfect for the corporate world, Moorhouse believes.

In sport there are also very good objective measures of success, like trophies and tournaments, and this can seem only of passing relevance to UK plc – industry awards being nice but not the most exact replicas. But, as Moorhouse points out, it's wrong to suggest that business lacks yardsticks of success: "Martin Johnson has a world cup to aim for, but can you really tell me that if you worked for a pharmaceutical company you couldn't set the objective of creating a life-enhancing drug?"

When inevitably he is forced to specifically discuss his stint in the pool, Moorhouse highlights lessons learned in 1984, not 1988.

"Losing the Olympics caused a big transformation in me. It made me change my approach, become more collaborative and find out why I performed well or not."

Opportunity is never enough

It wasn't always that way. Lane4 spent its formative years in a kind of limbo as the three founders – Moorhouse, a sports psychologist and a salesman – tussled with the shape of the business' core offering. (The name came from Moorhouse's sporting pomp: the fourth lane in the pool is usually allocated to the strongest swimmer.)

"[Our breakthrough] started from a chance encounter really," he says thinking back. "3M had commissioned a couple of sports psychologists at Loughborough University to help them improve the performance of their managers by training them like Olympic sports coaches.

"When I arrived at the university they were working on the 3M project and were short of funds. They had no idea about things like profit and loss, but it struck a chord with me and I thought we could make a business out of it. When the project was finished we created a case study and used that to develop interest from our first clients."

But Moorhouse found that opportunity – and taking advantage of it – is never enough unless it's backed up with hard graft and attention to detail. Happy clients remain the key to his success. The story of Lane4's development from then to now is one of referrals and the coming and going of senior managers between large organisations. When struggling supermarket chain Safeway became the target of buyout offers in 2004, the consultancy was hired to raise motivation, improve leadership and above all maintain the share price in what was to be a difficult year.

When Safeway was finally broken up and its shops sold to Morrison's, Asda and Tesco among others, the old Safeway management picked up senior positions at other big companies and rehired Lane4 for their training and leadership needs.

"Get your arse in a rented flat!" (Or, how to make your own luck)

Nearly 20 years on Moorhouse still struggles with the transition from sportsman to businessman. He can't quite let go of his watery roots. He has a "summer job" commentating on swimming for the BBC and can't help throwing in sporting metaphors to illustrate business scenarios.

When I ask him whether he feels lucky to have been successful in two independent worlds, he says luck accounts for about 5% and then describes a real life example of how you make your own.

"I was commentating for the BBC at Sydney and Sharron Davies was interviewing two swimmers, an American who had won gold and a British girl who finished five seconds off her best time. The American rattled off her preparation and training, while the Brit blamed her performance on the fact there were no 50-metre pools where she lived.

"I turned the microphone off and my co-commentator and I started screaming. She was from Newcastle, there's a pool in Leeds and one in Manchester – just move. Get your arse in a rented flat! You could argue she was unlucky for being born somewhere with no Olympic-size pool, but you have to question how much she wanted it."

CHARLIE MULLINS

A Plumber Who's Flushed With Success

Charlie Mullins thinks he's just an ordinary plumber who prides himself on a job well done. But his £16m turnover business and seven-figure salary have made him Britain's richest and most famous pipe fixer. His name is synonymous with the trade, and actors, musicians and businessmen clamour for his services. Witness the rise of Britain's first celebrity plumber.

Common sense

"Michael Winner is a real pain," laughs Charlie Mullins, the 53-year-old founder of Pimlico Plumbers, in answer to my question about his celebrity clientele. "He's the most difficult customer on our books – very hard to please. But if you can make a fella like that happy then you must be doing something right."

Mullins is talking from behind a big desk in his sparsely equipped office on the first floor of Pimlico Plumbers' 30,000 sq ft headquarters, based, confusingly enough, in Lambeth, South London. He is dressed in his signature shirt, smart trousers and branded tie and completes the look with an expensive Mod-style haircut.

Mullins is a salt-of-the-earth geezer. He speaks in a South London drawl which gives away his lack of formal education (by the age of nine he was skipping school to earn money with a local tradesman); he doesn't know how to use a computer and his mobile phone is a battered first generation Nokia: no colour screen, internet, GPS nor any other trappings of a modern handset.

But he is wise, logical and exudes commercial *nous*; perfect for a business he acknowledges is based on "common sense".

Plumber PR

Roger Moore, Daniel Craig and Brit Ekland are all customers. Photos of Mullins chin-wagging with this or that famous face are plastered all over the walls of his HQ. There are also letters of thanks and a book full of press cuttings applauding Pimlico's good work and the achievements of its employees.

Mullins is obviously making the most of his PR opportunities, which since partnering with Max Clifford's (also a customer) publicity machine are coming as thick and fast as water from a freshly repaired tap. A band formed from staff members has appeared on TV numerous times, while Charlie himself comments on anything from MPs' expenses to the merits of an up-to-date thermostat.

As Mullins points out: "You can be the best company in the world, but it's no good if no one knows about you. Hardly a week goes by when we don't get something on the telly and a lot of what I do now involves the PR side of it. There's no harm in promoting a good product."

"The best thing I could have done"

Occasionally his PR effort blurs with campaigning of the political kind. Mullins contends that jobs solve most of society's problems, including crime, homelessness and drug abuse. He is publicly lobbying the government to introduce a new system of apprenticeships that he believes will dramatically decrease youth unemployment and by correlation the nation's ills.

In fact, an apprenticeship is how Mullins started his career. He maintains it was "the best thing [he] could have done" because it gave him the skills and the confidence to set up his own business. A teenage Mullins impressed customers so much that when he finished his apprenticeship he was able to bring many with him to the new business.

The twin pillars of politeness and transparency

Having qualified he started doing jobs in the Sidcup area but it was not until he adopted the 'Pimlico' brand, inspired by an estate agents of the same name which became a regular customer, that he picked up business in Central London, allowing the business to flourish.

Only in the last few years has publicity become a major part of Pimlico Plumbers' culture, before which Mullins concentrated on the fundamentals of business: sales, service delivery and growth. It was his subtle blending of these ingredients, not media exposure, that made the company what is today.

Like many entrepreneurs within these pages, he saw a gap in the market. But unlike others, the gap Mullins slotted into was not manufactured from a great idea or prised open with new and untried technology. It was staring everyone in the face, and he can't believe Pimlico was the first to exploit it.

"It's obvious when you think about it. Plumbing is a very personal thing: you let a complete stranger into your house, so the service has to be right. He's got to be smart and polite, he's got to be able to communicate properly with the customer and he's got to do a good job without making a mess.

"That's how I approached the job when I was starting out and when I recruited people I told them how I expected them to act. We're clear about our pricing too and our charges are the second most popular page on our website because people want to know how much they're gonna pay.

"It sounds stupid, but that didn't happen before we came along. Communication is so important in this business but no one had done it right. I don't know why we were the first to approach things in that way, but we were," he says punching his hand to emphasise the point.

Reputation and recruitment

Being the best in the business means hiring the right people and as a major player with designs on geographical expansion Mullins must keep up his record of picking tradespeople with enthusiasm for Pimlico's values. The plumbing industry suffers from a reputation of being peppered with cowboys, which is partially justified, and he is wary of new recruits.

But the economic downturn means there are more skilled engineers looking for work and Pimlico's reputation means many head in its direction. This, combined with Mullins' boast that he can tell a "wrong 'un" within five seconds of an interview commencing, means he is enjoying a steady trickle of fresh talent.

Curiously, he is more interested in the way recruits present themselves and how they converse than their proficiency with a spanner, which can be demonstrated in certificates and experience. If they smell of alcohol (which sounds like it happens quite often), have nicotine-stained hands, are of shabby appearance or answer questions in monosyllables, Mullins doesn't want to know them.

Staying ahead of copycat competition

Pimlico Plumbers is coming under increasingly stiff competition from copycat outfits that have caught on to the benefits of transparency and professionalism. But Mullins is philosophical about the future and is glad of the rivalry: "If you want to be number one then you have to stay ahead of the rest," he points out, "and we're investing in making ourselves better all the time."

He installed tracking systems in his fleet of vans to make sure the nearest available engineers get local jobs, while his control centre is cutting-edge and strictly ordered to speed up reaction times.

But Mullins' favourite investment is his "noise machine"; a buzzer that sounds periodically to tell workers when to go on a break and when to come back.

"It cost two bob but it's worth an absolute bundle of money," he laughs, "Before we tried everything to get people in and out on time – even managers with whips. But now they act like robots when they hear it. I've never seen a device work so well. That's the sort of thing you should put in your book."

SIMON NIXON

Money-saver Turned Big Spender

With a personal fortune of £100m and business assets worth at least twice that, it's a wonder that Simon Nixon can motivate himself to do any work at all, let alone run three businesses simultaneously. But as the 40-something dotcom entrepreneur explains, retirement, however comfortable, is the last thing on his mind.

The biggest British dotcom success

Simon Nixon is Britain's most successful dotcom entrepreneur. As the inventor of the cost comparison website, he built his trail-blazing Moneysupermarket.com into a cash cow during the post-dotcom crash period when the rest of the internet was in flames. It floated on the stock market in 2007, valued at £850m and became Europe's biggest website listing to date.

Nixon himself pocketed £103m in the deal despite retaining a chunky 54% stake in the business, which he estimates is now worth between £250m and £300m. It is a personal success story that in financial terms dwarfs other British dotcoms, even big hitters like Lastminute and ASOS.

So it's annoying, then, that Nixon is so ruddy down-to-earth. He is easy to talk to and having spent two years as a 'corporate entrepreneur' communicating financial data to City shareholders, he is comfortable – though not in an arrogant way – discussing his pots of money and many investments.

The latest of the latter is SimonEscapes, a property investment and rental business offering wealthy 'staycationers' the chance to relax in multi-million pound holiday homes with five-star luxury but without leaving Britain.

"The majority of my wealth is still tied up in Moneysupermarket.com, so I need to invest money outside the business in a mixed portfolio to make it secure," Nixon explains in sincere tones. "Property is a good bet. When your money is in something intangible like the internet you want to put cash in something you can touch."

For someone of his wealth to talk in terms of 'securing money' is ludicrous, which the silver-haired business man acknowledges, but having cashed in his fortune relatively recently Nixon is yet to shake off the fear that he could still lose everything.

SimonSecures

So he has been trooping up and down the UK with an eye on the country's high-end property hotspots. His plan is to renovate old buildings or find new plots in prime locations, creating super-luxurious, multi-bedroomed accommodations and rent them out to play boys and girls for, let's say, £10,000 a week.

SimonEscapes' first property is Borth Cottage in Abersoch, North Wales; a modestly entitled castle which boasts dazzling sea views, a helipad and enough space for 12 guests to rub shoulders in comfort. There's also a cinema, hot tub, sauna, three living rooms…the list goes on.

But the jewel in the portfolio's crown is yet to be built. Arriving in 2011 will be the equally mis-monikered 'Little Palgarron' in Padstow. Described as "a glamorous glass-fronted property on Booby's Bay in Cornwall" the plot alone cost Nixon £4m, while the build will take the overall price up to £8m.

It's a figure you'd expect to pay for a listed town house in Mayfair, not a holiday pile on the west coast. But Nixon reckons he'll get £20,000 a week for it when Britain's rich and famous hear about its many delights.

It is surprising, given the large amount of money piled into his property business, that Nixon doesn't see SimonEscapes as his priority. And though he remains deputy chairman and major shareholder, his main focus isn't Moneysuperket.com either. No; the project he is really getting his teeth into is SimonSeeks, a travel reviews website start-up.

Growing a business

"SimonSeeks especially is potentially a big global business, I'm really focused on it. It's got to become a lot more successful than it is now before I'll be happy to go and look for other opportunities."

It is still brand new, yet it has received more than £1m in investment from Nixon's own back pocket and is attracting 1,500 visitors per day ("that's not very many," he reflects). The website will require four of five times that much money and won't break even for at least three years, but he is looking forward to the battle.

The website is as much a hobby as a business for the Nottinghamshire-born businessman. He is a fan of travel like he is of property and his decision to set up a dotcom having already worked the larger part of his career in one reflects his enthusiasm for his new cause.

Upon entering the site, users have access to a filtering system to help them find guides relevant to the type of holiday they enjoy, say a romantic trip in Paris or an adrenaline-fuelled jungle break in South America. Nixon rejects comparisons with Lonely Planet or Time Out, claiming that they reserve important information for the paid-for guides and give little away for free online.

"The difference is their guides are written by one or two people and we have hundreds of contributors, plus if you type 'Paris guide' into Google you'll get a load of excerpts and then a call to buy the book. They have to do that otherwise they cannibalise their sales," he says.

The community are the staff

Like Wikipedia, for example, SimonSeeks' content is produced by the public. But the way it builds content is different in several important ways. For a start there is a team of editors who check each guide against house editorial standards before they click the 'publish' button.

Secondly, it is attracting expert authors and even celebrities who want to share their travelling experience with the public. Thirdly, it offers a revenue-share model for contributors – who earn a kickback from cash generated through adverts and affiliate partnerships running across the website.

"The writers are incentivised to make their guides really accurate and high quality because we share half of any revenue that we generate for the guides with the writer," explains Nixon enthusiastically. "That also incentivises them to keep their guides up-to-date as well. Our community is incredibly important to us; in fact our community is our outsourced workforce. So we're paying them part of our revenue, they're our staff."

Personal needs and entrepreneurial deeds

"I set up businesses because I encounter a personal need for them. With SimonSeeks I wanted a source on the internet where I could just go and book a holiday very easily or get inspiration for, say, a romantic weekend in Europe. And there was nowhere I could do that."

Moneysupermarket.com was formed from the same basic principles as SimonSeeks: a personal need and a self-motivated solution. In the mid-1990s he wanted transparency in the finance market so people could get a fair deal on financial products such as mortgages, loans and credit cards. Nixon formed the website from an earlier business providing mortgage comparison software for brokers. The software, called Mortgage 2000, was simplified for public use and when in 1999 Freeserve announced it was rolling out internet access, he saw his opportunity to grow the business in a fast-growing online arena.

The hardest part for Nixon was getting the banks to play ball. For them signing up to a comparison service could mean being exposed as pricey. So they resisted offers to list their product lines until the website became so popular that it was clear that they would damage sales by not doing so.

From there, things just grew and grew.

KAVITA OBEROI

The Healthcare Consultant With a Heart

Brought up in a supportive yet traditional Indian household, Kavita Oberoi's entrepreneurial endeavours were both encouraged and inhibited by those around her. The secret of this millionaire's success is sheer hard work – that and a bloody-minded refusal to accept the status quo.

Conflicting influences

"You're such an inspiration," trembles an emotional Kavita Oberoi. "Because of my education, it's allowed me to run my own really successful business and it's made me a millionaire," she continues, trying to force back tears which are streaming down her face. "I've got a present for you: I've got £25,000…will you take it?"

Regrettably, this is not part of our interview but the dramatic and heart-warming conclusion to Oberoi's turn on Channel 4's *The Secret Millionaire*, which ran in August 2008. The former medical rep turned IT guru donated a significant chunk of cash to worthy causes in one of Birmingham's most deprived areas.

She changed her tune from the start of the episode. On receiving rations for the week she had reflected: "Why aren't people going out and working?"

Her views were the product of a comfortable upbringing in a traditional Indian family where females cook, clean and nurture, and men pay for the food on the table. During the programme she admitted never having set foot inside a tower block; "I've only seen them on TV," she says.

Oberoi's story is one of conflicting influences. On one side is her mother who fostered her education, and her father who founded a plumbing business and bestowed upon her an entrepreneurial streak. On the other are the customs of her religion and caste where women generally live un-enterprising lives.

The first female in her family to enter higher education, Oberoi received a first-class degree in applied chemistry from Huddersfield University. She chose to study there because she was not permitted to live on campus and needed a college she could travel to.

"And I wanted to do medicine but wasn't allowed to because by the time I finished I'd be 26 and nobody would marry me then," laughs a jovial Oberoi. "It was really hard getting through the four years because I was introduced to a lot people for a prospective marriage, but luckily I managed to hold them off right until the end."

Sacrifices for success

When she finally accepted an arranged marriage, Oberoi used all the entrepreneurial traits of negotiation, adaptability and, eventually, compromise to ensure she would be allowed to work for a living. Most people would baulk at the result: dual roles of housewife and co-breadwinner.

"It's the same in business; you have to make so many sacrifices to get what you want. What I couldn't deal with was being cooped up in the home 24/7, but it does mean that even now, even though I run my business, I have to make sure there's a family meal on the table every day."

"We've got to nail them"

Oberoi is 39 and has been running Oberoi Consulting, an IT training and business consultancy focusing on the healthcare industry, for about eight years. She's been in meetings all day and her phone is permanently ringing. She explains that Oberoi Consulting is in a busy patch, with joint ventures to tie up that could grow the company's turnover considerably. "You can see how stressed I am. We've got some absolutely crucial projects going at the moment and we've got to nail them," she says determinedly.

One of the newer link-ups is with Amscreen, a company owned by Lord Sugar which provides digital screens to the NHS. Two of his Apprentices, Lee McQueen and Yasmina Siadatan, work in the business. Oberoi is tight-lipped about the nature of the deal, but she's excited by the prospect of working with TV's foremost entrepreneur.

She is cautious too. For a start the project needs a little refining in her view, but more importantly she knows that strategic partnerships don't always work. Just a few months before our interview her business linked up with another firm, invested time and money in the relationship and at the last minute was abandoned by the partner.

"It's really important to get your commercial agreements put in place very early," she says, thinking back. "I had this fantastic idea and brought in a company, we developed the market and when it was all set they decided to run with it on their own.

"It didn't matter how much we fought them even though we drew up the legal contracts early on."

Personnel problems

The same applies to staff. One of Oberoi's regrets was her soft touch with employees in the business' formative years. Soon after going solo as a sole trader she landed a £500,000 contract with blue-chip pharmaceutical company Pfizer. Knowing she couldn't do all the work herself, she got hiring.

"Initially I used freelance people, which was a big mistake," she says. "They take away your knowledge and they don't have the same vision and passion and priorities because it's not their business."

She admits permanent and apparently loyal staff can cause problems too. Three months before our meeting Oberoi fired a senior member of staff who was secretly setting up against her. "The theory books say develop your staff, give them control and delegate. I let them manage a crucial product that has serious implications for the business. In the end they didn't set up the business only because I fired them before it got to that stage."

Multiple endeavours of an entrepreneur

Everything else is taken care of: the business is cash rich and, as a service-based consultancy, has no requirement for stock or raw materials. Oberoi set up and grew her business from her bedroom, so office costs were not a factor in the early days, and now she has a constant stream of clients in the NHS and pharmaceutical companies. The NHS is after all one of the biggest employers in the world.

The profitability of the business means Oberoi can reinvest returns in sideline interests. Despite the undulating market she chose commercial property as one avenue, because prices held up in the area of Derby where her business is based. She also hires out the headquarters for a little extra cash.

"It's one thing making money but how many people can make that money grow? You either make it grow or you lose it. So from the start I've been very keen, while the profitability's there, to reinvest," she says.

"Most entrepreneurs run a number of businesses at the same time. One should be the main revenue generator but there are other things that you can invest in which don't take up a lot of your time. You've got to keep to your core, but if you're investing in something like property, once it's done it's done."

SAM MALIN

Madagascar's Oil Man

Widely regarded as the founder of oil exploration in Madagascar, Sam Malin is leading the African island into the 21st century with mining, eco-tourism and bio-fuel projects. He explains how one man can hold such sway and how he balances progress with huge environmental and social responsibilities.

Oil man who doesn't drill

As chief executive of Avana Group and founder of Madagascar Oil, Sam Malin is every bit the oil man, yet his companies have never pulled any of the black stuff out of the ground. As a speculator, he locates and researches potential oil fields, proves that the stuff is accessible, then stands back and lets the drilling companies do their work.

The days of oil shooting geyser-like from the ground are behind us. Today, with easy-to-access oil fields drying up, the process of securing new supplies and developing technologies to access them is more complex, drawn-out and expensive. There's plenty of oil about but only a small proportion is available for consumption.

In short, oil is no longer a simple business. Finding resources is not the same as establishing that oil is recoverable at a cost that works. In addition, for every barrel that is extracted, mining companies must leave two or three barrels in the ground for technical reasons.

Bemolanga and Tsimiroro, the two massive Madagascan oil fields over which Madagascar Oil holds a licence, contain perhaps 3.5bn gallons of mostly heavy oil. To put that vast resource into perspective, the whole of the North Sea contains about 15bn barrels.

So you'd think they'd work like crazy to get it up, but it's not the case. Oil excavation is so expensive that companies go through painstaking checks before committing themselves. It could cost between $10bn and $15bn to drain the well of its resources.

From Leamington Spa to Madagascar

Malin, who holds a dual British-Canadian passport, was born in Leamington Spa, spent most of his formative years in British Columbia and studied geological engineering at Queen's University in Ontario, before returning to Britain for post-graduate studies at Cambridge.

After visiting the university careers advisor he was placed with US consultancy firm Arthur D. Little. As a junior consultant Malin was exposed to a range of markets and developed his interest in natural resources. Then, after serving with a series of companies in Paris and London, he got his first taste of Madagascar in 1994.

"I first got involved with Madagascar in 1994 with World Petroleum Consulting, a very grandly named Calgary company with two staff and me as a consultant," says Malin in a hypnotically light Canadian lilt. "I wasn't directly involved with the heavy oil fields on the island, but there was a lot about them in the briefing notes."

"I decided I wanted to do something with these oil fields that nobody, not even the Japanese company that my employers were working for, seemed interested in. In the period after, the fields were looked at by Hunt, the oil company that the TV show *Dallas* is modelled on, but by 2003 they decided not to proceed with further work."

Biding time and finding funding

For Marlin it was ten years of patiently waiting for his opportunity. He spent time as an advisor to the EU on international development in the area, looked at potential financiers for his plans and sought expert advice on how to make the oil fields marketable to the industry.

Funding for the project came from controversial Australian entrepreneur Robert Nelson and former billionaire Alan Bond, who famously went bankrupt in 1992 in Australia's biggest-ever corporate collapse, before being sent to prison for fraud five years later.

Malin was chief executive of the business for just two years before its hair-raising growth convinced him that it required a big team of professionals. Not before raising $300m in investment for the project (his main role was to raise finance) and bringing in Total as a partner on one of the fields.

"I stepped back from the day-to-day running of it basically because the projects were so big we needed to put in a team to get it to the production stage. Being a professional manager is not what I most like to do, I like getting the project up, running and financed.

"I remember signing my first $5m cheque, which was for some steam generators that pump into the oil fields. I remember thinking, 'this is getting serious'. Then I ordered the 250-man camp out in the field. The project simply became too sophisticated for one person."

DAME MARY PERKINS

Delivering on a Global Vision

Specsavers is the world's largest independent eye-care business with a growing base of 1,500 opticians and some 25,000 employees. Still a family business after 26 years, its co-founder Dame Mary Perkins is in no mood to retire and on the contrary has embarked on a course of aggressive global growth.

A family firm

As we talk in the opulent surroundings of the Central London hotel where she is a guest, I find it hard to comprehend that the softly-spoken sixty-something sat opposite me is a Dame Commander of the Order of the British Empire who presides over a business that shifted £1.5bn-worth of product in the financial year 2009-10. Looks, however, can be deceptive.

Despite its great stature, Specsavers is very much a family firm, founded by Dame Mary and her husband Douglas, with executive responsibility also shared by their three children. The family's eldest son, John, is managing director, having been promoted from finance director in 2007.

The business was established in 1984, just as the Thatcher government removed rules restricting the marketing of opticians' services, and has thrived by advertising its 'same glasses, lower cost' offering. Today it spends tens of millions of pounds a year on cross-media promotion under the slogan: 'You should have gone to Specsavers.'

The joy of joint ventures

Within a year of establishing the business in 1984 they had set up five shops in Bristol, Swansea, Bath, Plymouth and Guernsey. This,

Perkins tells me, established a base and a reputation upon which the business could launch its true strategy. Since then Specsavers has grown, in the vast majority of cases, through joint ventures with independent opticians.

The idea is simple: Specsavers relieves opticians of the onerous tasks of administration, accounting, marketing and IT, and in return the eye doctors enter into a 50-50 partnership with the mother ship and pay a management fee. They retain the profits, which are often enhanced under the bigger brand name, and can sell their shares at any time.

"Our structure is unique in our industry," Perkins assures me. "Optometrists are very good at their jobs but they don't tend to be very good business people. [With Specsavers] all these optical experts have to do is what they are trained for: see to the customers and look after their eyes. Everything else is taken off their hands.

"Quite often they prefer to do a joint venture than have a Specsavers open in the same small community, and in fact quite a few have made more money by converting to us."

Faced with a 'cake or death' scenario like that, most independents willingly succumb to the company's advances. And the decision is on the whole justified; Specsavers is yet to close a shop, and in 2009 grew its UK market share from 34% to 39%, far outweighing its closest competitor, Boots Opticians.

International expansion

Every week a handful of new Specsavers open their doors for the first time. Forty-five UK outlets are planned in the short term alone and Dame Mary tells me that while waiting for my arrival an alert popped up on her Blackberry announcing yet another successful launch.

Where possible, the Perkins family have also exported their formula for business expansion to overseas markets; first in Ireland, then Holland, Scandinavia, Spain and so on, until most recently the company broke into Australia and New Zealand, opening 200 stores in just 18 months.

While money isn't a problem, guiding the Specsavers brand through a collage of languages and customs can be. In Australia, for example, business continuity plans are just about unheard of, as are mystery shoppers, yet both are integral parts of the Specsavers strategy. In Holland, meanwhile, 'spek' means 'bacon'.

"Expanding overseas is not easy. The first country, now 12 years ago, was the Netherlands and on the surface it appeared the right place to go so we went in and from that experience we learned that culture is different in every country, however much they appear to be the same.

"In Holland you would never dream of setting up any retail outlet without a coffee machine and a person on hand to offer a cup. And a nice cup too. I did try a coffee machine in a UK store after that, but it was so much hassle because the stores are much busier and somehow the Dutch were tidier than us!"

The art of branding

She admits that persuading 1,500 venture partners to keep up with the parent company's latest colour scheme and shop layout is a subtle art, especially when the partners themselves are footing the bill, so the Retail Brand Development Team plots a course for slow, continual rebranding that revolves in seven-year cycles.

"Our customers will usually only visit every two years so you wouldn't want to suddenly alter the image. You want them to feel that they can trust you and they're coming back to the same place again," says Perkins.

"The optician partners pay for it, so if we said to the whole estate next year we're going to fit you all out and you're going to look like this, they'd say, 'Hang on a minute; I've only just opened and I want to get my money's worth out of the existing shop fittings'."

Unlike in the case of most billion-pound businesses, Specsavers likes to keep everything in-house, including processes like branding and marketing which are so often farmed out to agencies. A recent article in a trade magazine pondered whether this was a good idea, especially given the company's massive advertising budget.

Perkins thinks it is, and the company has invested heavily in marketing across the world. Each country has its own creative team headed by a director and different regions have different ads to suit the national consciousness, though they share common elements like photography which helps keep costs down.

"The fact that we do our own advertising is one of our key differentiators because our people are very much involved in the business, whereas an agency will work hard on your account, but you'll go back the next year and you've got a different team there and it's a learning process the whole time."

Through the looking glass

While Specsavers is far and away the number one eye-care brand in the UK, competition is hotting up. Boots' merger with Dollond & Aitchison proved its commitment to the sector, Tesco is a new entrant and small internet retailers have begun taking chunks out of the market.

Perkins famously clashed with one of this new breed, Jamie Murray Wells of Glasses Direct, when he fought to win a place on the General Optical Council, despite not being a qualified optometrist. Perkins led a campaign to prevent it happening and called for only "candidates with the interests of hands-on, professional practitioners at heart" to be eligible.

The combination of value for money, an ever-present brand and a unique structure have made Specsavers the giant it is today, but having reached critical mass and with growth accelerating globally, Perkins is still excited about the future. The company is only the third largest optical company in the world, she says, so there is motivation in becoming number one globally as well as fighting off pretenders to the UK throne.

KEITH POTTS

Careering Towards His Online Goals

With first-mover advantage in the online recruitment space, Keith Potts and family have built up a massive internet empire backed by one of the biggest names in global publishing. But with geographical growth and market share still available, Potts is not stopping there.

Trading since school

Keith Potts is a jolly character. Speaking with him over a coffee in a London café, I can't help noticing that most of what he says is accented with a chuckle or a full-on laugh. For him, business is fun and he wants everyone around him to share in the experience – including me. He is enthusiastic and knowledgeable and despite going through two equity sales earning him "about £9m" his relish for the cut and thrust of business is undiminished.

Like many people who make it as an entrepreneur, Potts has been trading in one way or another since school. Like Sir Richard Branson (among others) his first taste of enterprise was on the playground, renting Top Trumps and other games to friends for two pence a lunch break.

At university, instead of getting trashed in the student bars, he formed a sandwich business to feed the hungry stragglers after campus eateries shut up shop. Before that he washed cars for extra cash.

He now runs a handful of businesses but his primary venture, Jobsite.com, is part of a sprawling network of recruitment (and related) websites worth more than £100m. Apart from his "day job", Potts also owns a carp farm, a safari business in Zambia and is chairman of a company providing software for football coaches.

From employee to entrepreneur

It's odd, given his entrepreneurial streak, that Potts started his career as an employee. For years he worked as a software designer for large aviation companies building flight simulators. Having created these "£10m games machines" the job meant sketching out mathematical models of runways and forwarding updates to the simulators via Telnet, an early vehicle for transferring data between computers.

Without realising it, Potts was using an early form of internet protocol – or the web to you and me – and his experiences with emerging online software formed the basis for the creation of his internet jobs board in 1995.

Working with his brothers and sister-in-law he started a business giving people and companies access to the internet, sometimes handing out modems as an incentive to join. The business diversified with the development of the internet and the team began creating websites for corporates, but soon the focus returned to Potts' jobs board.

"It was a chicken-and-egg scenario"

"My middle brother used to put candidates and vacancies on that recruitment system, match them up and send letters to companies telling them he'd found matches for their needs. That was his business. So I took that model and put it online and we launched it in September '95."

At the time there were only 40,000 internet users in the whole of Britain, so the website targeted those with an interest in technology jobs. As the web popularised, Jobsite (as it became known) spread to other niches, gradually building a portfolio of recruiters to serve the burgeoning demand from online job hunters.

"It was a chicken-and-egg scenario; we'd got a job board with no candidates on it and no vacancies," Potts chortles. "So we teamed up with a few recruitment agencies and asked them to put their adverts on for free. We got IT candidates predominantly. From there it grew and grew like you wouldn't believe."

Selling at the right time

In 2000, at the height of the dotcom boom, Potts and his family of co-founders agreed to ring-fence some of the business' value for themselves. The founders had always ploughed profits back into the business, never taking dividends, and after five years it was time to secure some cash.

For strategic reasons they sold a 49% stake to a recruitment business called Manpower. The deal valued Jobsite at £17.5m – an 11.5 multiple on its revenue. The generous nature of the deal reflects the headiness of the boom; had they sold even a year later the multiple would have been much smaller.

"Nobody gets it right every time, but that was a good example of selling at just the right time."

The growth of Google

At the same time Google was still a start-up having been formed late in 1998. When it eventually became clear that it would become the UK's most popular place to find information, Potts switched his attention from Lycos, Yahoo and Netscape, learning about search engine optimisation (SEO) and Google AdWords.

"I would spend all night sussing out what Google was thinking about the world and I would manipulate pages to get Jobsite right to the top. When Pay Per Click came out, I knew exactly what the effect was going to be.

"Most people didn't get it for about two years, but I remember having this eureka moment when we worked out that you could stop doing the SEO bit as much and just buy your way to the top. Jobsite was in exactly the right place; no competition at all and we absolutely creamed it."

Jobsite spends around £100,000 on AdWords every month and has developed a database of 65,000 key phrases used by people searching for jobs online. The results point to one of 90 websites in the portfolio.

Potts has also experimented with viral campaigns online, with varying degrees of success. However, they still have "hundreds of holidays sitting in the cupboard" from a failed free hotel-trip promotion.

A rocket

In 2003 Manpower came to the conclusion that partnering with Jobsite was no longer part of its strategy and sold its stake to the Daily Mail and General Trust Plc, publishers of the *Daily Mail* and a host of other newspapers, websites and radio stations.

"Because we're highly entrepreneurial we need to feel that we own the business and DMGT very much do that. They're very skilled at acquiring companies but leaving that company in a *modus operandi* that makes everybody feel that they still own it and run it."

The deal put a rocket up the Jobsite brand. The backing of a corporate entity of DMGT's stature allowed it to grow quickly with a large marketing budget incorporating cross-media advertising and sponsorships of large music and sporting events. The site also made a series of acquisitions to compliment its organic growth.

Potts is hungry for more and looking at new countries as well as emerging social media tools to spread the brand.

"We need to be at the forefront of everything that's happening at the moment – take Twitter, I'm all over it like a rash!"

IAN POWELL

The World's Most Powerful Accountant

As chairman and senior partner of PricewaterhouseCoopers, Ian Powell is responsible for 77,000 people in a company that stretches from Norway to South Africa, from Portugal to the eastern tip of Russia. Being that far up the chain it's a wonder he doesn't get dizzy. But, as he explains, management is not about preaching from on high.

Talking to 16,000 individuals

PricewaterhouseCoopers (PwC) is the biggest professional-services company in the world. Formed with the merger of two British accountancy companies in 1998, the firm employs 155,000 people worldwide and generates some £28bn in annual revenues.

It is headquartered in a globular, beetle-like building at the north-western end of Hungerford Bridge in central London and Powell's office is a long, smooth lift ride from the marbled reception at ground level.

But the big man is not hidden away in an ivory tower. Surrounded by other desks and the buzz and tapping of industrious fellow accountants, his squash court-sized office has a glass wall overlooking the shop floor. The outer wall is glass too, affording him a stunning view of the Thames, Charing Cross and the Millennium Wheel.

As chairman of the UK practice his main responsibility is to the people who work beneath him. His challenge is to focus the minds of PwC staff towards a common goal by formulating a simple strategy that 16,000 pairs of eyes and ears can understand.

"I remember when I led a team of 16 people in Manchester," says Powell. "I knew their families and their hobbies and what they did at the weekend. Now it's very different. I get in a lift and everyone knows me – it just feels a bit strange.

"A long time ago I did some media training to prepare me for TV appearances. One thing really helped me: when you go on the news and you talk to eight million people that's too much for the brain to accept, so you break it down and imagine you're talking to each person individually."

Powell uses this approach in management as well as media. Establishing a one-to-one "emotional" relationship is extremely important when you're speaking to staff or customers.

The Nike of numbers?

As a service business, the company's reserve of tangible assets is tiny. There is no plant, factory or warehouse brimming with stock and no machines of any great value. What it does have in spades is the intangible skill of its employees and the attractiveness of its clients. PwC is a people business and communication is therefore central to its success.

Powell was voted in as top boy by the firm's partners in July 2008 and has spent his time convincing people that PwC should be an iconic brand like Nike and Adidas in sport, or Microsoft and Dell in computing. "According to our research, iconic brands – not necessarily the biggest ones – tend to be the most profitable. The best people want to work for iconic organisations and customers want to buy from them. I don't know if we'll get there and we can't judge it ourselves, but it's a real goal," says Powell determinedly.

"If you keep doing the same things that got you there, one thing's for sure: you won't stay the best for long. Our ambition must be greater."

The difficult decisions

That said, the realities of business in 2009 have not been lost on Powell, who wants to be straight-up with his staff. A few weeks prior to our interview he distributed a video message telling them of a freeze on pay increases. It's better to deliver a clear message from the top than to let the rumour mill churn, he believes.

Powell is a business-restructuring specialist by trade and no stranger to difficult decisions or decisive action. As his career developed throughout the 1990s he was handed increasingly large businesses to turn around or carve up, including Marconi, Lehman and NTL, which culminated with him being called in after the spectacular MG Rover Group collapse of 2005, where 6,500 workers at the Longbridge manufacturing plant in Birmingham lost their jobs.

Administrators were called in to the car manufacturer the day after Parliament dissolved for a general election. The situation was therefore political dynamite and it generated even more media attention than a large corporate collapse usually would. Not even the pope's funeral, or Prince Charles' second marriage, could keep events off the front pages, and Powell was in the middle of the media maelstrom.

His first trip to Longbridge "was enormous, like going to a major sports event. Several hundred media were already camped out at the plant and there were only four of us. Despite everything else going on in the world we were the number two news item that night," he remembers.

"When you're in the eye of a storm like that it's easier sometimes, that's how we got through it, but the media interest was almost disproportionate to the business. We had to be careful because PwC needed protection in the heat of this intense and explosive situation."

Powell is satisfied with his company's role in the break-up of MG Rover, which culminated in manufacturing rights being transferred to Nanjing Automobile Group in China for a reported £53m. Despite PwC's more recent infamy for making thousands of a client's staff redundant by text message, Powell is particularly proud of PwC's support for the many people who lost their jobs at the plant.

The company organised an open day where former staff could get help signing on, find out their legal position and receive advice from employment experts and union representatives. "Even the Rover chaplain was there," he recalls.

Meanwhile, local employers were invited to set up a jobs fair and began conducting interviews on the spot. "We worked hard to make it as painless as it could possibly be," he adds. "A few of the workers thanked me personally, which was really gratifying because we knew they were hurting."

"A nimble gorilla"

Unlike the MG Rover of old, PwC is in rude health. Despite, or because of, the recession of 2009 the firm's counter-cyclical services – such as those supporting distressed companies – are going great guns and Powell expects turnover to approach levels reported in 2008, itself a record year.

He puts the company's momentum down to its entrepreneurial traits; particularly its ability to adapt in changing circumstances. Spotting emerging trends, most recently to do with sustainability and the environment, PwC has quickly developed a team of 800 experts to serve client needs in the field. "We like to think of ourselves as a nimble gorilla," he jokes.

DOUG RICHARD

TV Entrepreneur and Tech Start-up Guru

Doug Richard knows an awful lot about starting businesses. He's responsible for a number of successful and (he'd be the first to admit) not-so-successful launches both in the UK and in the US. Now the Californian entrepreneur wants to help you avoid the common mistakes he made as a first-time starter-upper.

A fire-breathing angel

We're chatting in his luxurious private club in London's Portman Square. Doug is in a jolly mood, enjoying his role of 'investor without portfolio' since his main business interest, Library House, closed in late 2008.

Today he is a business angel investor and – through his latest venture, School for Startups, a not-for-profit course for uninitiated entrepreneurs – mentor to scores of would-be Doug Richards. It gives him the flexibility he craves and the freedom to pick and choose projects close to his heart.

Though now an angel, he has been mostly known in the past for his fire-breathing, having appeared as one of the mean investors in series one and two of *Dragons' Den*. His clipped, rational delivery and hawkish approach to investing contributed to the BBC show's early reputation for being a bit nasty.

But the immediacy of the TV format didn't suit Richard's real-life cerebral and analytical investment style, and having given the nod only twice in 12 episodes, he opted to leave the show in 2005. Contrary to his on-screen persona he is a people person and off-camera never invests in entrepreneurs he couldn't have a beer with.

"*Dragons' Den* has accentuated the idea that everything has to happen at that one moment, but my own investment style is the antithesis of that. It's my view as an angel investor that I should work with people before I invest to make sure that we can work together.

"I think more business angels should put their time in for free before they invest. At the end of the day, it's just a few hours out of our lives. It can be incredibly valuable for the entrepreneur and both parties' risk goes down enormously; the alternative is two strangers wondering if it's going to work out."

Entrepreneur and investor

All of Richard's fingers and toes are embedded in numerous entrepreneurial pies. Today he's particularly keen on two main investments: a futuristic new scooter and, less glamorously, a business and accounting software service for small businesses.

But as well as backing entrepreneurs Richard has been known to start the odd business himself, first in his home state of California then more recently in the UK. His first business was ITAL Computers, co-founded with his brother, which basically involved selling computer parts.

"We were essentially traders in that business," Richard admits. "One regret is that I didn't realise that we were sitting on what was potentially a very large business. We were out for a quick buck at that time so we didn't concentrate on building the business. When we sold it, it was a modest business and we sold for a modest amount of money."

Richard's relationship with his brother was tested by their entrepreneurial partnership and when they exited ITAL he resolved to keep family and business separate from then on.

In 1991 he founded 3D software company Visual Software with the proceeds from the ITAL sale and in 1995 sold to US-listed business Micrografx, later becoming its CEO. Richard sold Micrografx in 2000 to Coral and moved to the UK, founding Library House, a company selling data on businesses and investments, and eventually finding fame through *Dragons' Den*.

When credit started to crunch

Richard describes Library House's closure as his major failure in 2008. The financial data company was heavily reliant on big City-based companies, such as hedge funds and private equity groups, for its revenue and when the credit crunch gripped money markets that year, customers fell away in droves. Income dried up in just three months and the business went into administration.

"It was regrettable because I built a reputation in the media based on Library House," he admits. "I was always quoted as founder of Library House in the press, for example. So when I closed it my reputation suffered, even though in the same year I had a couple of nice exits which made up for the financial loss."

Another of Richard's business interests which suffered in the credit crunch is Trutap, a mobile social-networking application which connects phone users through a range of services including instant messenger. The business missed a funding round at the end of 2008 and was forced to cut headcount by 80%.

Richard is confident that the business still has legs. It has amassed a large and growing following, notably in developing markets, and the technology has won respect in the tech media. Later versions of the software are elegant and could justify putting the old team back together, he says.

"Its timing wasn't particularly great because we preceded the iPhone by just enough to miss that particular boat. But having said that it became fairly successful in its own right and we're in the process of restoring the team and growing it again. It's not my best start-up, I admit, but it's certainly not my worst."

The Kafkaesque approach of government help

On balance it's hard to miss the conclusion that Richard's business successes, his first three endeavours, were all founded, built up and sold on American soil, while the UK played host to his flops. Is it possible that territory has something to do with the varying fortunes of his businesses?

Richard is better qualified than most to make this assessment. Not only has he run multi-million pound businesses on both sides of the Atlantic but in 2008 he published a report backed by the Conservative Party which condemned government support for British entrepreneurs.

His main grumble is with the support structure itself, which spends billions of pounds 'signposting' support groups: "It is as though we have created a labyrinth of services that are so complex that we have had to create a further service whose primary remit is to decipher them," his report reads.

Government support for small business is such a large and complex effort that small businesses have been set up with a central goal of obtaining government funding.

"They also claim that one of their roles is to provide advice, except they're civil servants," exclaims Richard, becoming animated at the chance to speak on one of his favourite topics. "At what point did they decide that they were experts? Except they're not experts and they're tendering a lot of this out.

"Who are they tendering it to? People in the profession of business support. What made them experienced at it except for the fact that they at some point started doing it? Then they realise that, at 3,000, there are too many support groups, so they promise to reduce it to 100. Why 100? How do they know there are 2,900 that don't fit the bill? It's all a bit Kafkaesque."

Richard calls the system "a pretence of productivity" and "a classic replacement for productive activity". It's all headlines and very little actual progress, and it has made him cynical. Richard claims he is apolitical but is helping the Conservatives because they are Labour's successors in government and as such have to get it right first time. He reckons they will need all the help they can get. For the entrepreneurs themselves, his School for Startups is traversing the country offering sensible advice for pre-start businesses.

CRAIG SAMS

Millionaire Foodie With a Conscience

Together with his wife Josephine Fairley, Craig Sams has been a pioneering eco-entrepreneur for more than 40 years. The Green & Black's co-founder launched a broad range of businesses in fashion, restaurants and, lately, carbon capture; but always made his millions with a clear conscience.

From amoebic dysentery to macrobiotic dining

It took a bout of serious illness on his travels in the 1960s to steer his good nature into projects that would make him a multi-millionaire.

On a trip to Asia and the Middle East, Sams was struck down with a double dose of hepatitis and amoebic dysentery. The latter receded in time but the former condition left him, in his own words, "devitalised and weak".

Upon returning for his final year at Pennsylvania University where he was studying economics, Sams was introduced to the macrobiotic diet: a predominantly vegetarian eating regime that incorporates whole grains, vegetables, fruits, legumes and seaweeds.

Revitalised with the benefits of eating well, his interest upgraded to enthusiasm when on a trip to New York he visited a macrobiotic restaurant that had opened up in the East Village: "When I walked into the restaurant the hairs stood up on the back of my neck and I knew this was what I wanted to do," he says.

He ditched plans to join the Peace Corps and teach English as a foreign language, upped sticks and moved to London, where his family had been based since 1960, to found a macrobiotic restaurant of his own.

"I was basically trying to make money so I started three businesses at the same time: the restaurant, an ethnic fashion import business [also inspired by his travels] and a retail outlet for organic produce," he recalls. "But we started supplying whole foods on a wholesale basis too and pretty soon this became our focus."

The rough and tumble of peanut butter

Sams enjoyed a monopoly in the early days but increasingly powerful challengers began making life difficult for Whole Earth Foods, the wholesale business which he kept and renamed (whilst gradually selling on the fashion business, restaurant and shop). They were soon stealing market share and bullying suppliers. On top of this the product range was easy to copy and to sell at cheaper prices.

"We realised that there's nothing distinctive about brown rice and beans to be able to brand them, so we narrowed our range down and concentrated on peanut butter and jam. Gradually a new range emerged with soft drinks, pasta sauces, ketchups and salad dressings. The idea was to appeal to people who were eating brown bread and rice and had that kind of commitment to quality, but then would spoil it with naff pasta sauces."

But even in its new form the business was not immune from raids by competitors. In 1989, Sun-Pat, then owned by Nestlé, made a big push to corner the peanut butter market by invading the whole-food space. The effort proved abortive, partly because the 'whole-nut' product lacked quality, but Sams admits, "it caused a panic".

With its mega-bucks, Nestlé could afford to flog its organic copycat with a green lid even when it proved a timid rival to the Whole Earth Foods version, which by that time had become the UK's second favourite type of peanut butter.

"As it happened they failed miserably," Sams remembers. "Their peanut butter was terrible; they had something called 'whole-nut', which sounded something like Whole Earth. It was pretty pathetic; the nuts were rancid so it tasted foul. We couldn't believe our luck. But they soldiered on; it was Nestlé so they didn't have to worry about losing money for three or four years."

Such was the growth of his brand that Sams sought new organic peanut suppliers and on a trip to Africa he chanced upon a group of farmers who grew organic cocoa beans as well as the peanuts he was after. Negotiating with the French owners of the farm and tasting a few sample chocolate bars that they produced, he resolved on a new venture – which became Green & Black's.

Hot chocolate

The new business represented a change of pace for the husband and wife team. When they sold their last remaining shares in Green & Black's it was turning over £22.5m and demand was so great that they had to use technical financing solutions and equity sell-offs to pay for stock and distribution.

The name was a simpler affair – the product of a 15-minute brainstorming session. The couple ruled out obvious and unappetising names such as 'Eco Choc', preferring a moniker that would evoke traditional confectionary. Drawing inspiration from Callard & Bowser, they settled on Green & Black's. The 'black' covered the rich chocolate content, and the 'green' covered the ethical aspect without – as it were – ramming it down customers' throats.

They already had an in with the supermarkets because of their existing peanut butter and jam business and getting the chocolate in front of a buyer was fairly easy. Legend has it that Lady Sainsbury was personally such a big fan of the new product that Sainsbury's became the first to take it on.

"Nobody else had 70% chocolate, there was nobody else that was organic.

"Most of the things I have done in my life, going right back to Afghan coats, I've been the only one in the market and I prefer it that way," Sams chuckles. "Inevitably competition comes along. They always compete either by being more efficient or by having a crappier product. An awful lot of chocolate got wasted by people trying to knock us off our perch."

Outside help

Nevertheless, interest was growing in the gap filled by Green & Black's and the founders knew it would not be long before a business with more money posed a real threat to their market leadership. The only solution, as they saw it, was to sell equity and in 1999 they relinquished 75% of Green & Black's to a group of investors who made their money founding and selling the Covent Garden Food Co.

New managers were hired, including sales and marketing professionals with backgrounds at GlaxoSmithKline (then SmithKline Beecham) and Burger King. They brought all the strategic, tactical and market awareness skills that the brand needed at that stage in its development.

Equally importantly, they brought a big bag of money and threw it at the business. Prior to the investment, income from sales went straight back into working capital, such was the demand for stock. Now the business had £2m to spend just on marketing, and with the subsequent sale of Whole Earth Foods they had even more cash to invest in building the fame of Green & Black's.

It meant that when the husband-and-wife team finally sold it to Cadbury in 2005 the business was ten times more valuable than six years previously: "That 25% of the business that we finally sold in 2005 was worth many times more than the 100% of the business we had at the beginning of 1999. So that was the trade-off for giving up such a lot of our business," Sams contemplates.

'The other woman'

Sams sold his Cadbury shares in 2009 and now has no legal or financial link to the brand, though is very happy with how Cadbury have maintained Green & Black's integrity within the wider organisation.

Today he runs three small businesses: a bakery, a health centre and Carbon Gold.

Like so many successful entrepreneurs of a certain age Sams refuses to retire despite his wealth, opting instead to scale down his business interests and focus much of his efforts on campaigning for good causes, including lobbying ministers and MEPs to include soil as a recognised carbon sink.

That and the important work Sams carries out on his allotment, which he admits is "the other woman" in his life. Such is his love of gardening, the millionaire entrepreneur felt the need to name his garden: 'Lottie', appropriately enough.

ROB SHREEVE

Playing Host to Entrepreneurs on the Move

Having worked under Sir Richard Branson – the acknowledged high priest of enterprise – for ten years and subsequently run a business (great idea, bad timing) during the dotcom bust, Rob Shreeve reckons he's on to a sure thing with One Alfred Place: a temple of enterprise where business meets pleasure and gets on famously.

Glass walls and blue skies

A cursory glance at One Alfred Place, the address housing the members' club of the same name, tells you nothing about the delights that sizzle within. The giant, domineering glass structure that One Alfred Place calls home, though it rests on a whole street of traditional Victorian properties, looks like it could have been airlifted in from a science park. Nor will peering through its transparent ramparts provide any new clues. The ground floor is disconcertingly sparse, with just a desk and some columns interrupting the bright and barren expanse.

Take the short trip to the second floor, however, and everything becomes clear. It's as if you have been moved to an entirely new building. Space is still a theme – the club offers 10,000 square feet of legroom – but the décor is different, comfortably composed of mixed and matched armchairs, sofas, unfussy low tables, various lamps, scattered cushions and £1.7m-worth of modern art.

One Alfred Place is shaped like a giant doughnut. The 'circuit' is big enough to stage a foot race and many of its rooms offer a view onto the inner courtyard which it hugs. Endless windows line the walls and together with the whitewash paint-job create an effect that is uncluttered, cheerful and breezy; perfect for 'blue-sky thinking'.

Shreeve is extremely busy on the day of my visit and the smiling receptionist suggests I fetch a drink in the club's restaurant, which I discover is plenty bigger than many standalone eateries. Food is a big deal here, as Shreeve himself later explains; more so than the late-night drinking which some of its competitors specialise in.

Breeding ground for business

Shreeve arrives delivering a stream of apologies and suggests we take a booth for our meal. Despite his entrepreneur's uniform of suit and open collar shirt, he looks a bit like the Radio One DJ John Peel: similar face, facial hair and even accent – though I should acknowledge that Shreeve is a good few inches trimmer than his late doppelganger.

It's one of a few things that connects Shreeve to the music industry. A more substantial link is the club's group of investors, which includes Phil Collins, Pink Floyd drummer Nick Mason, Genesis manager Tony Smith, and Mike Rutherford of Genesis and Mike + The Mechanics.

"And all our investors use us," says Shreeve proudly. "That's one of the great things about us from their point of view: instead of sticking your money into some remote investment or some fund that's going to push it into derivatives that none of them understand, this is an investment that they can touch and feel and come and use."

We sit, order some food and Shreeve switches to 'media mode'. He's talked about One Alfred Place a lot since it opened in 2008 and the story of its creation rolls easily off his tongue. "When I started this place I saw it, truthfully, as just a physical space; a solution to the problem of working in London and not wanting to sit in hotel lobbies or in a club which didn't have the usual technology that I expect to have when I work.

"What I completely underestimated was the networking potential and the value that the members give to it, that and the number of businesses that have already started organically in this building by people who are getting together because they meet each other and know each other.

"It's not necessarily businesses that wouldn't have happened had they not been members; people have ideas and they would probably have realised them anyway, but they've been able to do it in partnership with other club members because they've found them.

"And I wouldn't be at all surprised if it hasn't facilitated ideas that would have been on the backburner had they not suddenly found themselves sitting opposite somebody who could solve their problem."

"Who you know is more important than anything"

To bolster late-night business, the club has extended its hours until 11pm and plays host to regular events. A few nights before my visit alumni from Harvard Business School were quaffing booze until close, while not long before that former Beach Boy Brian Wilson performed a set to publicise a new book.

It has also enjoyed visits from former *Dragons' Den* star Doug Richard, *Big Issue* founder John Bird and the artist Peter Blake.

It's a who-you-know business all right. Since conceptualising One Alfred Place, Rob Shreeve has used his network to transform the business from idea to reality. Robert Devereux, who ran some of Virgin's biggest media brands while Shreeve was MD of Virgin Publishing, is today chairman of the club.

"I've come to the feeling that life's too short to do business with people you don't like. If the idea's strong enough, you'll be able to find people that you like. Getting on and respecting the people you work with is more important than anything, because it has tangible business benefits anyway. There's too much time wasted on politics if you're working with people who are fighting each other all the time."

Learning from the past

There's very little crossover between book publishing for Richard Branson and being a front-of-house founding CEO of a hospitality business. But Shreeve says the same fundamental business rules apply, making his business past relevant to what he's doing now.

The same, it could be argued, applies to the business Shreeve left the Virgin mother ship to run. EU Smart plc, which provided digital certificates as proof of age and ID, was well ahead of its time and aborted because the product was difficult to grasp in what were early dotcom years.

But the idea was ingenious: authenticated online identities which would have allowed people to open bank accounts, sign legal documents or prove their age buying alcohol or in chat rooms for children. All you had to do was take your passport into a post office and receive a digital stamp or code to be used online.

"It was a great idea, but nobody knew what digital certificates were. Nobody felt they needed them; none of the suppliers wanted to go digital, they didn't trust it yet, they wanted to stick to good old paper and envelopes and ten-page forms and the punters didn't know any better.

"It might have cost the government a couple of hundred million, but you would have had an authenticated community of people, able to transact much more securely with each other. Parents could have felt more secure about their children's online safety. They could say, 'Who are you? I just want to see your ID', like showing a passport."

Shreeve was brought in to curb the founders' spending. They had raised £22m and spent £10m on practically nothing. Shreeve spent an additional £4m trying to make the product work in an era that wasn't ready for it, including developing a system that allowed people to transact online without credit cards.

Finally, after hitting numerous brick walls, he canned the project and gave the shareholders back their remaining money. The experience, while ultimately a failure, taught Shreeve to conserve cash and give people what they want – at the time they want it.

One Alfred Place fits this latter criteria. It's less like a bar than some members' clubs and more like a social, relaxing environment than some of the more austere establishments; not to mention the cafés, train stations and libraries that are the entrepreneur's alternative for working on the move.

Shreeve and Devereux plan to take the concept global, starting with other major British cities like Edinburgh. But will it fly? Comfy yet professional, with great technology and infrastructure, complemented by a sumptuous assortment of food and booze; I'm tempted to say 'yes'.

GIL STEYAERT

Custodian of Adidas' Olympic Dream

As managing director of Adidas' northern European territories, Gil Steyaert faced a huge challenge from the recession that hit sales of consumer goods, and an equally sizeable opportunity with London's Olympic Games. Despite the former, Steyaert predicts the latter will make Adidas the UK's market leading sports brand.

"The best time for big ideas is in bed"

Steyaert, a 46-year-old executive with a marketing background, joined Adidas from cereal makers Kellogg's in 1999 and has risen from senior country-based positions to become managing director of the UK, Ireland and Benelux region in 2003. He is French but lives in Britain.

I meet Gil at Adidas' PR nerve centre in Covent Garden. Unlike the corporate headquarters it is dimly lit and smallish, cluttered even, giving it a cool edgy vibe. After a short wait in reception, Gil appears and waves me into an office.

A corporate bigwig, Steyaert is different to the entrepreneurs I have interviewed. He is methodical in his answers, the product of media training, unlike greener bosses who rattle through their views without pausing for breath. He gives off a natural and calm authority, though this composed nature is contradicted by his loud stripy shirt.

His main role is the overarching management of people and processes.

"It means I spend perhaps 90% of my working life in meetings," he says, not joking. "Allowing time for strategic thinking is more difficult. The best time for the big ideas is the toilet and in bed, certainly bed in the morning is when I think of a lot of plans."

A sporting brand

At the time of our interview Gil's plans all point to 2012 and London's Olympic Games. Notwithstanding its move into high-street fashion during the 1970s and 80s, Adidas is a sporting brand first and foremost and has been closely involved with major sporting events (notably in football and athletics) since it first started making shoes.

In 2007 Steyaert was part of the team that won the company primary sponsor status for the Games, alongside BT, Lloyds TSB and EDF Energy. Under the deal it will invest around £100m in sponsorship funds and provide 70,000 uniforms for officials and volunteers, as well as equipment for the Paralympics.

"The Olympic Games has always been huge for Adidas, along with the World Cup. It's one of the two legs of credibility," he tells me. "We've been in the Games before anybody else. The way we've been in the Games has been different in different times with different types of sponsorship.

"Recently in Beijing and now in London we wanted to be a partner of the Games itself, Beijing because it was China and it was a political way to install a lot of stores. London is slightly different; London is a big centre in the world in terms of trends and fashions and we want to be there in 2012."

Adidas switched from being a manufacturing business to focusing on marketing during the 1980s when the cost of making goods in Germany began eating away at profit margins. Now the business, like its main rival Nike, spends vast resources positioning their brand.

Steyaert allows that the two sporting leviathans are "fighting with the same recipe" – in other words they have sought-after product ranges that are fashionable as well as sporty, both have top manufacturing and distribution infrastructure and both have a global footprint. The only outward differentiator, therefore, is branding.

People sponsorships can be a significant driver of sales in this context. Remember what Michael Jordon did for Nike in the US and David

Beckham for Adidas in the UK? The top brands, not just in sport, but gaming, confectionary and grooming jostle for the biggest stars to promote their best-selling lines.

Multifaceted fundamentals

But, as Steyaert describes, even these big personalities won't sell more stock unless the product designs are right, the quality is there, new lines go swiftly to market in the shops, and the whole process is carried out efficiently.

"There is from time to time a winning, significant different brand driver that could actually push sales higher [such as Beckham or Jordan], but it will go down to not one big campaign but a lot of smaller practical things that will make the real difference. In our market it's individual execution in each country that counts.

"It's different from a lot of other industries. Look at Apple and mobile phones: one item, one campaign shifted things significantly. In other markets, one innovation – Fusion or Mach 3 – draws a lot of the company's focus. We are tennis, football, hockey, cricket and rugby. We are so diverse, so multifaceted, that we don't have any one thing that can make the difference."

In a recession, it is more important than ever to consider these nuts and bolts carefully. The latest accounts available, for the second quarter of 2009, show Adidas' global sales down 8%, while the higher cost of materials squeezed gross profit margins by 5%.

"The good news is that we did not see any fundamental deterioration in our business since publishing our first quarter results."

Running against recession

Adidas was fighting the 2008/09 recession before it even began, with spending freezes across parts of the business. Budgets for entertainment and travel were cut and while there were no reported job losses, rises and bonuses were put on hold. The company also sought to help its retail network overcome their problems.

"I very quickly went to one or two key retailers in the country who were wobbling and made sure I helped them as much as I could to survive.

"They are our point of sale; customers need retailers, they are the way to the market so I invested time and money to make sure that they are surviving first and then have the facilities to get through it."

But Steyaert also knows when to get tough with retailers. When discounters started stacking Adidas products high and selling cheap, Steyaert moved to protect the brand. In a joint move with Nike, Adidas began reserving premium product lines for non-discounters such as JJB Sports and JD Sports who in return agreed to meet standards of presentation and display.

Steyaert believes his skills lie in "strategic thinking and acting" and also in being good with people. "I dare say they like to work for me and respect me. You can't impose on people to follow you," he says.

Does he enjoy the limelight that comes with a high-profile position? "I'm not 100% comfortable with it – I doubt anyone is. When it comes to public profile I'm in the pack, not ahead of it, but I wouldn't classify it as a 'tier one' role in my job," he smiles.

ASHLEY WARD

The Saviour of Wharfedale

Ashley Ward's near-30 year career as a serial chief executive has left him bruised, battle-scarred, sceptical and wiser for it. He has achieved remarkable successes: the revival of a tired yet loved British brand and a stock market flotation valued in the hundreds of millions of pounds being two notable ones. Yet impatient moneymen and predatory colleagues have tarnished what could otherwise have added up to an unbridled succession of business victories.

Master of all trades

Partly due to a few unfavourable experiences, and partly because of his addiction to new things, Ward's CV reads like a menu from an all-you-can-eat buffet. There is no career path as such, more a game of hopscotch from one business to the next. Ward has been a successful racing driver and a less-successful actor as well as a businessman, and since electing to focus on running companies in the mid-1980s, he has continued to exhibit what might almost amount to capriciousness in the colourful range of projects he has taken on (everything from car alarms to stereo speakers and headhunting).

We grab a coffee in one of the small shops that line the lanes running parallel to his large Victorian offices on London's Regent Street. Before we can start the interview in earnest he picks up my mobile phone and starts tapping away at the keys. He checks out a few of its features, decides he has seen enough and promptly saves his number in my call list. "There," he says flatly, "if you need anything else, you can reach me on that number." Then, pulling in his chair, he starts talking.

"I made every possible mistake"

Ashley Ward has founded or been parachuted into seven companies as CEO. His first business, which he started, sold financial modelling software for now ancient Commodore PET and Apple II personal computers – the first units to be mass-produced for private buyers during the late 1970s and early 80s.

In the early days the company did fabulously well. The directors made good money and the business floated on a junior exchange for smaller companies that became a trailblazer for today's Plus Market. Such was the excitement surrounding the listing of a pioneering technology company that Sir Nicolas Goodison, the then-chair of the stock exchange, was called in to manage investor interest in the business.

But soon a catalogue of errors, misfortunes and not a little deceit from advisors and suppliers caused the business to fall apart. "I was 27 when I started the business and 30 when we floated it on the stock exchange," he remembers. "I was looking for investment money and I was drawn in by 'clever people' who attached themselves to me. The next thing I knew they were on my board."

"We diversified too much, we grew too quickly and some of our products had been pirated in America which really hammered our market. Then the software was effectively wiped out by a better product called Lotus 123, which came along in 1984. We couldn't compete with Chinese manufacturing because we were manufacturing in Wales. We were also a retailer of IBM PCs and the margins on those disappeared in 1985."

Eventually, a licensing mix-up with one of its chief product lines sealed the business' fate and Ward put it into voluntary liquidation, clawing back what money he could from the failed venture. "I think you have to recognise when the writing's on the wall and if you can get something out of a situation, get something out of it," he says.

"We owned his conscience. I knew he was our man forever."

Now in-between businesses, Ward proceeded to job as a consultant and while working in this capacity for a small merchant bank he was offered the chance to buy Wharfedale, the iconic British stereo speaker brand. "The bank had a mandate to sell Wharfedale and they asked me if I wanted it. I explained that I didn't have the money, they told me not to worry about that. So they found the financial backing and I bought Wharfedale."

Wharfedale had been wrecked by its former owners and its star had faded in the consumer consciousness. But in four years Ward restored it to its former glory, acquired other businesses to beef up the brand and rolled it into a bigger quoted company, securing its future. He says the secret to the turnaround was listening to the market and finding people who could become 'brand ambassadors'.

"I discovered that the most influential people were the kids on the stereo shop floors, because you'd buy whatever they recommended, and the reviewers in magazines. We hired some reviewers to work as consultants in the manufacturing process. They assumed that they had contributed to the finished products and so rated the speakers with five stars every time.

"Then we paid 19-year-olds from the shops to come to the factory and wind one of their own coils for a speaker. We put a little plaque on the front and they would go away with a pair of speakers that cost us all of £35, but we owned his conscience. I knew he was our man forever."

Greatest achievement and biggest failure

Ward's other great achievement was also his biggest failure, when he took telecoms software company Orchestream from pre-revenue to a market cap of just under £1bn, qualifying it for FTSE 250 status. But in 2000, technology stocks were headed in one direction and one direction only. In 2002 Ward was fired by his board because of dwindling turnover and a tumbling share price.

"I learned about dysfunctional boards at Orchestream. I really needed some support and guidance with that company but I got none; I only got criticism and hostility from the venture capital directors and shareholders. In the end the help I got was a hatchet between my shoulders and trip from the eighteenth floor the quick way," he says a little ruefully.

The problem for Orchestream was its client base. Telecoms companies had a horrible time during the dotcom bust and three-quarters of those using Orchestream software went bust. But the product, bought by Oracle in 2006, was perfectly viable and is still going great guns today. Customers now include Vodafone and AT&T.

A true businessman

Ward has had a number of other successful ventures: with Cray Communications, for example, which he took over, increased its sales, sliced it up and sold it on in instalments to Intel and Cable & Wireless. He sold his car alarm supply business for three times its buying price and he pioneered pre-digital messaging devices which were used widely in industry.

Ward is a truer businessman than many entrepreneurs who have generated much larger personal fortunes. His many and varied experiences of business boom and bust have etched upon his brain the mistakes that generations of entrepreneurs repeat time and again – and the important lessons. And while he would have preferred the benefit of more support and better outcomes in some of his ventures, his familiarity with the dark side of business makes him the perfect mentor for future generations.

MARK ZALESKI

The Sage of Silicon Valley

Despite the humid and wet conditions in London when I meet Mark Zaleski, he is resplendent in three-piece suit, breast-pocket handkerchief and, crucially, umbrella. He's tall with a forthcoming, casual demeanour that exudes the sort of unfussy confidence often displayed by those who've done all right for themselves.

The merits of being anally retentive

Zaleski is English but based in Belgium and when I interviewed him he had just finished a spell as chief executive of Paris-based DailyMotion.com, the super-cool video-sharing site. Although only in his 40s, Zaleski has held director-level positions in international businesses for 20 years and is a survivor of the dotcom bust. "You know you're getting old when you have stories to tell," he jokes.

Like many successful people, Zaleski's rise to business stardom began with a stroke of luck – but he had to make his own, too. At a tender age he became station manager in a Brussels branch of Federal Express, the parcel delivery business, just as the company entered one of the most successful periods in its history. "If you were average you could grow as fast as the business, but if you were better you could grow faster," he explains. "It was a genuine meritocracy and you had every opportunity to do well – so I did." Zaleski was one of the leading lights in this period of growth and was soon put in charge of Fed Ex's Asian division.

Its ability to target near-perfect satisfaction rates with new technology made Fed Ex great to work for. "Fed Ex was anally retentive when it came to getting things right," Zaleski recalls. "Because you could measure it, you could manage it." (Fed Ex was IBM's second-biggest customer after the US government.) The work systems this technology allowed them to create "were what set the business apart from everyone else. It took all the guesswork out and I loved it. It's better to work for a strong company because you can focus on growth rather than fire-fighting," he smiles.

Banishing Del Boy and becoming the Web Van man

In 1994, already with senior management experience under his belt, Zaleski got a call from AC Nielsen, the market research company. In his own words the role he was offered was to "commercialise statistics" or in layman's terms, make better returns for a 70-year-old company staffed with academics who equated sales people with Del Boy.

Having impressed at Nielsen, Zaleski received a call from a Silicon Valley headhunter, who eventually recruited him to California dotcom start-up Web Van, the online grocery delivery service which was to become one of the dotcom boom's most impressive collapses.

Unlike many dotcom casualties, Web Van had a valid business proposition. It offered customers the luxury of ordering groceries online and having them delivered in half-hour time slots. The idea remains big business today. In the UK, delivery service Ocado has a turnover approaching £500m.

Nor was the problem to be found in the management team's CVs. On paper the Web Van board was a who's who of commercial geniuses, from Louis Borders of Borders bookshops, to former Anderson Consulting (now Accenture) chief executive George Shaheen. Investors included Yahoo and Goldman Sachs.

Zaleski slotted in as chief operating officer just as the business was getting off the ground. It had already won seed and Series-A funding, and when he arrived in 1998 employed around 40 full-time programmers.

"In two years our business went from 40 to 4,000 people, we raised hundreds of millions of dollars funding with just a few phone calls and when we finally came to float the business the initial public offering was 18 times oversubscribed.

"Normally when you do a pitch it's to a few people in a quiet room. We were pitching in the biggest conference halls that Goldman Sachs or Merrill Lynch could provide – and there were still people listening from outside in the hall.

"In the end the hype went to some people's heads. Our finance director said we would be profitable in six quarters, which with $850m invested and only $80m turnover was impossible."

Inevitably cracks started to appear and disagreements at board level ground progress to a halt. Meanwhile, like other dotcoms, the business was frittering money away. Borders insisted on recruiting expensive developers; distribution centres were built at $35m each; and it had palatial headquarters, which mimicked those of a multi-national blue-chips.

"We were convinced we'd be worth £100bn, that it was our God-given right, so our investors put pressure on us to build our footprint as quickly as possible and get first-mover advantage. But we didn't even know if the model worked, I really wanted to *prove* the concept first."

In the end, he wasn't allowed to. Web Van spent $1bn in 18 months and folded in 2001. It was a victim of the prevailing dotcom sentiment: throw enough money at a project and eventually the business will come good. Before jumping ship he devised a plan to restructure Web Van, taking it back to basics and building from its core offering. After 12 months of discussion the board agreed, but by then it was too late.

Fire-fighting and Polish escapades

Unable to achieve traction with his 'softly softly' approach to growing Web Van, Zaleski opened his ears to new opportunities and was again headhunted, this time as CEO, to fellow dotcom era giant QXL.

QXL, or QXL ricardo as it became after an acquisition in 2000, was the ill-fated British rival to eBay which was popular in parts of the world outside the UK and US. Zaleski joined, "right in the nasty bit of the dotcom boom", when the business was burning through £1m a week in its bid to outgrow eBay.

Both businesses were buying up smaller independent start-ups as part of their growth strategy, but such a busy spell of purchases took its toll in terms of cash flow and the operational difficulties of merging new operations and locations. Zaleski's job was to bring all of the acquisitions together, stabilise the business and eventually turn a profit.

QXL's stock price had lost 99% of its value but Zaleski maintains that the business was turning the corner when his work was thwarted. He claims the managing director of QXL's operationally profitable Polish business took the business from the umbrella company: "Poland was the perfect developing market for online auctions and it became half of our business," he remembers.

According to Zaleski's version of events, the Polish MD and his lawyer transferred ownership of the business and were eventually prosecuted for breaching professional ethics. The charges were dropped and the management team settled out of court to win back the Polish business, having spent millions on the legal battle.

With the business remerged, Zaleski resigned as chief executive and left the business in 2007, though he retained shares and "did very well" when the business was de-listed from the London Stock Exchange and sold to South African media company Naspers early in 2008 for just under £950m.

A posh YouTube

Since then Zaleski's plan to "sit on a few boards and do some investing" took a temporary backseat as he volunteered to help professionalise the fiendishly popular, though at the time loss-making, DailyMotion.

According to online ratings website Alexa.com, it's in the top-100 most popular websites in the world, but measures introduced by Zaleski made it legitimate, legal and commercial as well as popular.

Simply, it's a posh YouTube and it doesn't get sued by content owners any more. Unlike most other video-sharing websites it has a 'fingerprint' authentication system so if someone lays legitimate claim to a video, it cannot be uploaded by someone else. If the content isn't fingerprinted but still infringes copyright, Zaleski reckons it will come down within the hour.

Thus media businesses like Warner, Disney and Viacom can protect their work against theft and are prepared to have content appearing on DailyMotion that is free for the user. It also opens doors to high-profile events like the Raindance Festival and to temporary pre-premier screenings of films.

THE

RULES

Starting a Business

Make sacrifices for your first clients
Adrian Moorhouse, Lane4 (HR)

When Adrian Moorhouse first founded Lane4 with a sports psychologist and a salesman, he lacked a business plan and, as an unrecognised business, had to fight for his early clients. His first customer was a British airport in need of a management-training programme.

After five presentations the buyers were still not convinced they should take a chance on Lane4, so Moorhouse offered them a performance-related price structure. First clients are always the hardest, and offering unusual incentives is a good way of getting them to choose your business.

"We asked for their worst people, the people they thought could never change, and we promised to motivate them. We asked for half the money upfront and then the other half if they felt we did a good job. It went really well, even when they gave us people who didn't want to do any learning. It was scary but we got results."

Online is not easier than bricks and mortar
Sarah Beeny, *Property Ladder*, Tepilo.com

It's a common misconception that online businesses are easier to start and grow than bricks and mortar ones. They are actually very similar, except that instead of a physical shop you have a website – which, by the way, can be just as expensive to run.

Sarah Beeny, creator of two dotcoms, found that out the hard way. Instead of launching her first website MySingleFriend.com and seeing it take off immediately, she found herself phoning friends and begging them to upload their details to the site.

"Dotcoms are a lot harder than you think. You need a fantastic website; I'm really proud of Tepilo – I didn't build it so I can boast about it. What I didn't realise with MySingleFriend is that you have to constantly update it to keep it relevant or it will come crashing down. Don't expect to build a site and just leave it there.

"MySingleFriend is really popular and it's successful, which is so exciting. But I have to say it was slow at the start; I had an image of it taking off really quickly and everyone using it, which is why I'm a lot more relaxed with Tepilo."

Research web-development companies thoroughly
Syed Ahmed, *The Apprentice*

Syed Ahmed had a nightmare with developers when he created a website for his first business, IT People. So much so that he founded a completely separate business, Get Launched, to help entrepreneurs avoid the same trauma.

"I created Get Launched because of the pain of setting up a business when you don't have all the contacts. In the course of having my website developed, I quickly learned that what other people need is a painless, one-stop shop. After we had it all in place our company flew pretty quickly."

Get a motto
Ajaz Ahmed, AKQA (marketing)

AKQA founder Ajaz Ahmed says that when he started his business he lacked the up-to-date equipment the firm is famous for today. He believes this was made up for by the founders' commitment to its founding principles: innovation, service, quality and thought.

From the outset the group agreed they would represent these values in everything they did. Although these qualities were never written down, or even articulated explicitly to clients, they have acted as guiding principles to this day and reflect the firm's continued commitment to quality.

"Our business needed to represent those four principles without us making a big song and dance about it. Those values are why AKQA evolved from a scrappy start-up to a large independent agency."

Make sure you are ready to trade
Anthony Ganjou, Curb (marketing)

When Anthony Ganjou founded Curb, a creative advertising agency that utilises the natural environment in its work, he waited a full eight months before pitching to prospective clients. He thought it vital that the business first build a full-service offering before showing advertisers what it could do.

"We help advertisers convey their message in a striking way that is natural, yet stands out from the environment, be that sand sculptures, crop circles or 'sea tagging'. I needed to be able to offer a range of these media to clients from the word go because I wanted Curb to look like an established business straightaway.

"Our employees were putting the supply chain together, because we didn't want to start without being able to deliver everything that we do. We wanted to work with the big boys from the word go and this preparation meant that we could."

Steal your first customers
Brad Burton, 4Networking

Like many people who start businesses, Brad Burton knew that his first customers would come from rival organisations. Unlike many start-ups, however, he went after them in brazen style, making it abundantly clear who he was and why he was stalking business-networking meetings.

In a flurry of guerrilla marketing Burton leafleted and canvassed local business people, convincing many of them to leave their networking groups and join the embryonic 4Networking for its first meeting. Having secured 72 attendees Burton never looked back.

"I handed envelopes to people. Inside it said, 'Good Morning?' and then listed the reasons why they should come over to us instead.

"I admit I just basically spammed people because I had no money or resources. But it was very smart spam that looked like it was written just for you. People were talking about me – good and bad – but those who hated me four years ago are all over 4N now."

If you want to plant a tree, plant a tree!
David Gold, Ann Summers

David Gold believes it's never too late to start a business. Older people have more life experience and are in many ways less likely to commit basic business errors, he says. Plus they have every chance of seeing the business mature.

"When I was 35 years of age I wanted to plant some trees at the bottom of the garden because beyond us there was going to be a development. My wife said to me, 'You're not planting trees, they'll take forever to grow'.

"I thought, 'Sod it, I'm gonna plant some trees'. So I planted half a dozen at the back of the house. She died a few years ago and after the funeral I looked out of the window and there was a row of magnificent trees and they looked stunning. So I say this to you: plant the bloody trees."

There is no magic formula for start-ups
Deborah Meaden, *Dragons' Den*

As an investor and mentor to a string of up-and-coming entrepreneurs, Deborah Meaden has unearthed some common misunderstandings held by people starting businesses. The most widespread, she says, is the belief in a universal formula for business success.

People regularly ask her for the 'secret' to becoming a wealthy entrepreneur, and she explains that it doesn't exist. For Meaden, an idea with potential, hard work and good judgement are the fundamental building blocks to building a sustainable enterprise.

"I get the feeling that when people ask me how to become successful they want me to say A, B, C, D, bingo! If only it were that easy. While you can't draw up the template for a perfect entrepreneur, there are definitely some common traits.

"People hope for a mystical answer, but actually I don't think business is that complicated. It's hard work, you have to have good judgement and be on the ball all the time, you've got to be effective too, and I don't actually believe that everyone has it in them.

"It's part of this pop culture, I get young people telling me 'I want to be a millionaire'. Being a millionaire is not a career; it's an outcome if you're clever and work hard. It's the result, not the actual thing you do. I ask them 'How are you going to do it?' And they reply that they don't know."

Get cosy with your market
Doug Richard, *Dragons' Den*

For Doug Richard, the most important thing people forget when they start a business is market research. Entrepreneurs must know that their product or service will be in demand; but too many people trust a gut feeling instead of getting out there and testing the market thoroughly.

"I'm forever telling people with start-ups to make something people want. And people say 'of course', but when I ask, 'How do you know?', then frequently they don't know, they believe. They haven't talked to prospective customers and they haven't measured the size of the need the customer has that they're replacing.

"They haven't worked through the logic of the proposition in adequate detail to persuade me there's enough room for a business to exist. They're all caught up in the excitement of having spotted a gap. Sometimes gaps exist because they should. So that first question should take up a lot of your time."

Grab all opportunities
Kanya King, MOBO Awards

A chance encounter with a high-powered media executive gave Kanya King the leg-up she needed to get her MOBO Awards a television audience. But the meeting was a blessing and a curse, as she was given just six weeks to put the inaugural show together. King is not one to shrink from a challenge, however, and she took her chance.

King's advice to other start-ups is to grab opportunities when they arise, however remote the likelihood that they will come good and no matter how much work is involved. The fact that MOBO exists is testament to her dedication and perseverance.

"I always believe that you should campaign for opportunities and when you get them you have to grab them. That's what we did. In six weeks we had to assemble a production crew, get a venue, and find available artists that were going to support us; it was an incredible effort. It was a tiny team but we were very passionate and we believed in it."

If they say you can't do it, prove them wrong

Kavita Oberoi, Oberoi Consulting (IT and healthcare)

When Kavita Oberoi was turned down for a promotion it proved the incentive she needed to strike out on her own as an entrepreneur. Less than 10 years on and she's running a multi-million pound healthcare IT consultancy. She says self-belief was the key to getting her started.

Having taken the decision to start up on her own, Oberoi surveyed her market and looked for opportunities. Fortunately, a new piece of tricky government legislation affecting doctors gave her the scope to start her consulting business.

"At the time I left, some guidelines had just come out and I found that the GPs were struggling with the implementation, and the first step to implementation was finding the patients on the computer and then putting the strategic plan in place to manage them. They couldn't do those first two steps and that was where I came in."

Never miss an opportunity

Keith Potts, Jobsite

Keith Potts runs the successful UK recruitment website Jobsite, but he also has fingers in several other entrepreneurial pies. From football coaching software to mirror-carp farming, his business interests cast a wide net. But possibly the most bizarre is the Potts family's 90% stake in a safari park.

"In 2004, we took our father back to Africa and we stayed at Norman Carr Safaris. Typically for us, we looked at this thing from a business perspective. We talked about whether we could get involved in some sort of equity stake; put the business on the web, get more traffic and more bookings.

"We spoke to one of the managers and they said that funnily enough they were trying to sell it last year. So we spoke to the owners and they said for the asking price at the time we could buy the lot. So we acquired 90%, left the director with a 10% stake and he became a partner."

You don't need to be original to succeed
Lord Bilimoria, Cobra Beer

Do not be afraid to start a business in an established industry, says Lord Bilimoria, founder of Cobra Beer. He believes most businesses are started because entrepreneurs see a need for their product or service and that it is passion, not originality, that makes success more likely.

"The essence of the idea, I believe, is that it has to be in some way different or better. It can be an existing product, but do it differently, do it better and change the market place that you're going into.

"You've got to be passionate about what you're doing. Invariably it's because you're passionate about something (good or bad) that makes you want to start a business. For me, it was my dislike of fizzy lagers, and particularly how badly they went with Indian food, and my love of beer, particularly real ale."

Get a vision
Mark Zaleski, DailyMotion

Mark Zaleski, a serial CEO who has lead some of the world's biggest dotcom companies, argues people need to be clear about their objectives before they start up in business. People motivated purely by money are most likely to fail, he says, and most that develop strong businesses have a clear path from the beginning.

"Some people go into business saying, 'How do I make a lot of money?' As opposed to creating something that people want and have fun doing it. Even if you have a mediocre idea, if you have good people around, you will be 'successful' – though you can define success how you want.

"You'll have an enjoyable life too. If you start out saying, 'I want to make this or that amount' the chances are you won't make it and you'll be miserable doing it.

"Ask yourself what you want to get out of being an entrepreneur. Do you want to lead an army of people or build something you love and keep innovating? You might think you just want to enjoy it – it's your right to scale it how you choose. Businesses can become like a big HR exercise, with you worrying about Sally in accounts' sick leave record rather than the product and the plan."

Start a business you love
Martha Lane Fox, Lastminute.com

Martha Lane Fox loves starting new projects. For her, the best stage of a business' life is at the beginning when the challenge is to transform a concept into a business.

But she maintains that entrepreneurs must have a passion for their new business, because once the novelty and excitement of the start-up phase has worn off, it is your enthusiasm for the product or service that will keep you going.

"Find where the passion is; you may have a brilliant idea but you may not feel passionate about it as a user. That's really important because it's hard work when things go wrong or when you're raising money and you have to fall back on being excited about what you're trying to do.

"The only reason I'm interested in starting things is because I have a passion for them. Not everyone feels that about their business, but I have to like the product at the consumer end and the feeling that you get when you love a business is quite extraordinary."

Get some experience while you learn
Max Clifford, PR

Max Clifford's advice for people starting up in PR is to 'just do it'. That particularly applies to people studying marketing and PR. He says there is no substitute for practical experience and mixing practical with theory gives you the added benefit of earning while you learn.

"While you're doing the theory, find a local shop opening and say that if they give you £500 you'll contact the local radio, papers and TV. You're learning and you'll save them £5000 on advertising.

"Just do it; you're making contacts and figuring out good angles. Most PRs say you should be hidden behind the scenes, but being out in front has worked very well for me."

For inspiration, do something unusual
Michelle Dewberry, *The Apprentice*, Chiconomise

When Michelle Dewberry stopped working for Alan Sugar, she found that for the first time in her life she had no specific plans. Seeking inspiration for what she should do next, Dewberry hopped on a plane to New York. It gave her the inspiration to start a new business.

"When I won *The Apprentice* I should have been happy, but I wasn't. I just thought what do I do now? What's next? I wasn't happy in a 9-to-5 job and it really threw me.

"I took time out and got on a plane to New York to work out what I wanted to do. I contacted *Glamour* magazine and asked if they wanted me to blog about this new phase in my life, and they signed me up. I had a great time, met some amazing friends and made business contacts and I came up with Chiconomise."

You don't need to understand 'entrepreneur' to be one
Peter Jones, *Dragons' Den*, Phones International

By the age of 12, Peter Jones was technically an entrepreneur. He founded his first proper business at 16 and by 20 was well on his way to becoming a millionaire. But for the first few years he admits he had no idea what an entrepreneur was.

"When I was 12 or 13, just starting out as an entrepreneur, I honestly didn't know what it was. I know Richard Branson is going to hate this, but when I was younger I looked up to him. But he seemed so much older than me, which hasn't changed today.

"I started my first business when I was 16 and started another one when I was 18. By the time I was 20 I was well on my way to building a successful company – and that's when I knew what entrepreneurial meant."

Industries are always evolving
Sarah Beeny, *Property Ladder*, Tepilo.com

With her new property trading website Tepilo.com, Sarah Beeny is trying to shift the market for home buying and selling away from estate agents and onto the internet. In doing so she is helping to shape the future of the industry. In 20 years' time all houses will be bought and sold this way, she says.

"I started Tepilo.com for the same reason I started mysinglefriend.com. Simply: there wasn't (and isn't) a very good alternative. You either buy through an estate agent or you go to slightly weird classified sites. People don't go to estate agents to look for a house any more. If the buyers are online then why aren't the sellers?

"It's because they can only do it through estate agents. The big sites are only a small proportion of estate agents. And I thought, what if you don't want to pay £10,000 plus VAT for an agent? Some people don't, they'd rather upload their own details.

"It's a modern way of selling houses that would have happened 100 years ago had the internet been invented. There has been some reaction from the industry, but interestingly they have been personal slights, rather than comments that the site isn't a good idea."

Find a need, start a business
Simon Nixon, Moneysupermarket.com

When Simon Nixon starts a business he almost always follows the same formula. His last three businesses – Moneysupermarket.com, SimonSeeks and SimonEscapes – were all motivated by a personal need that was not being served at the time.

It's an important set of questions every entrepreneur should ask themselves before they start up in business: Do I need something? Do other people need it too? Why is it currently not being catered for? Can I do it myself?

"Moneysupermarket happened because I wanted to see transparency in the financial markets. I wanted to compare the lowest credit-card savings and insurance quotes. I did it for me and I thought that it would be good for the people out there just like me.

"SimonSeeks was again my own requirement. I wanted an online source where I could book a holiday very easily or get inspiration for, say, a romantic weekend in Europe. I wanted to key in my requirements and receive back a big list of guides on what to do and where to go, so I made it happen."

Focus on cash flow from the start
Syed Ahmed, *The Apprentice*

Having set up and run IT People, Syed Ahmed had two years experience of getting a new business off the ground before appearing on *The Apprentice*. His biggest challenge in that time, he says, was keeping control of his cash flow.

"I experienced setting up a company from scratch, making all the mistakes, dealing with debtors, creditors, staff and payroll.

"To be honest it's not what you expect when you start up – you think you've spent something during the month and when you look at a bank statement it's something completely different, but I loved the process and I learned to keep the books tighter as I went along."

Plan from the beginning
Dawn Gibbins, Flowcrete

Dawn Gibbbins didn't write a business plan until eight years after she co-founded Flowcrete, her floor-manufacturing firm. She believes creating a plan galvanised the business and was the beginning of its growth curve. Today, her advice is don't delay when planning your business' future.

"I think the key thing in business is get your dream down, get the plan of how you're going to achieve that dream and just keep measuring, making sure you're getting there. As an entrepreneur you've got to get all your people believing that dream."

Remember the downside
Rob Shreeve, One Alfred Place (business club)

When you start up in business, be realistic about the threats you face as well as the opportunities, says Rob Shreeve, founder of One Alfred

Place. It's one of the key lessons he learned from Sir Richard Branson when he worked for Virgin: always assess the downside.

"The lesson I came away from Richard with is this: despite his buccaneering sort of persona, the first question he would always ask about any venture or big investment is, what's the downside? Assessing the downside is a good lesson, I think, because it's at least as important as the upside.

"It's all very well projecting and planning the positives but unless you know what the downsides are you don't know what your risk is. So, always project the downside and having recognised what the downside is, look at the idea, assessing whether you think it's a good one and if you feel in your gut it's the right thing, just do it."

CUSTOMERS AND COMPETITORS

Never overburden your business

Ajaz Ahmed, AKQA

As a pioneering business in an emerging industry, AKQA's website solutions were in high demand throughout the late 1990s and into the dotcom boom at the turn of the century. But while some competitors snapped up any work going, Ajaz Ahmed retained his small, high-quality customer base and resisted the temptation to go for quick growth.

Ahmed says that in most cases would-be customers were glad to get an honest answer; that the order books were full. The alternative might have been getting into problems later on with too many clients demanding work from too few AKQA employees.

"The dotcom crash took out a lot of our competitors. At the time I would have weekly meetings with my team and they would criticise me because I refused to take on work from the dotcom businesses. But I had seen these bubbles before with software and hardware. Think of the companies that were legendary in the 80s and 90s that don't exist now.

"For me, the dotcom bubble reflected that, so we wouldn't work with firms that didn't have a solid business model; we focused on blue-chips."

Keep stock levels plentiful

Ashley Ward, NEXEC partners, Wharfedale, Orchestream

With most retail businesses one of the worst things you can do is run out of stock. Customers want a broad range of products and they want them to be available instantly. Ashley Ward learned this lesson quickly when he bought a business selling car alarms.

"With car alarms you had to have the products in stock all the time – it was the days when all car alarms were retrofitted. The dealer would get a customer who'd decide the model and they'd say come back tomorrow; if you couldn't deliver the item by 10am the next day so the fitter could fit it then you didn't get the deal.

"All models in stock the whole time. I learned that from the guy that backed me. He owned a jeans retailer and his philosophy was 'every brand and size of jeans all the time' – regardless of what it does to your stock-turn – because you never want the customer to leave the shop without a pair of jeans.

"Accountants will say you have to turn your stock seven times a year, but you should always have products available. The people we sold the car alarm business to literally destroyed it by trying to get their stock-turn numbers up. They messed it up. They should have kept our philosophy – it worked."

Be prepared to educate your customers

Craig Sams, Green & Black's

Craig Sams founded Whole Earth Foods in the 1960s to sell macrobiotic foods to health-conscious Londoners. The health food industry was still developing at the time so Whole Earth was one of the first businesses of its type, meaning Sams had to work hard to generate customer interest.

"We had to do a lot of education. We hosted cookery and shiatsu classes and we had macrobiotics experts over from Boston to give talks on the subject. We rented a house where people could go to get immersed in the philosophy. We printed all sorts of recipe leaflets telling people how to do it and sold copies of a book called *Zen Macrobiotic Cooking*. It all helped to build interest in our products and to shift customers' mindsets in our favour."

Most important of all, understand your customers
Dame Mary Perkins, Specsavers

For Dame Mary Perkins, the most important thing new businesses should do is get to know their customers. Even today, Dame Mary enjoys paying the odd visit to individual shops and chatting with the customers who pass through. She says it's an excellent way to evaluate business performance.

"You've got to know that there's a market out there, so get to know your customers first and foremost. Stay in touch with them, too, because they change. This is why we brought in designer glasses. We knew there were people out there who wanted a designer name and wouldn't come to us because we didn't have them.

"I prefer to go into a store, sit down and talk to my customers. They don't know who I am, so I always get to hear what people honestly want to say. I much prefer that to focus groups, where all too often people come up with answers they think will please you."

Don't fear change
David Gold, Ann Summers

David Gold says he wished he could have owned Woolworths five years before the chain went bust in 2008. He believes its demise was caused by a failure to adapt to changing customer trends and that a 'we've always done it this way' mentality caused it to fail.

Having helped build Ann Summers into a wildly successful retail business, Gold is no stranger to customer loyalty. But he maintains that doggedly sticking with the same formula year after year is far from the best way to ensure customers keep coming back.

"The Woolworths collapse was quite a shock to everybody, although I have to say I think the recession was only the final nail in the coffin. Woolworths started to go bust 30 years ago and they fiddled with their systems but really didn't move into the 20th century, let alone the 21st.

"There was a great case for change in the whole philosophy of it and they just couldn't bring themselves to do it. I don't know why; maybe it was shareholders saying 'we don't want to change, we've always done it this way' – how many times have I heard that? It may have been customer loyalty. But that customer was someone who shopped there for 50 years, and five years ago she died."

Be prepared for sceptical customers
Doug Richard, *Dragons' Den*

Having launched and developed successful businesses both in Britain and America, Doug Richard is well placed to talk about the varying attitudes of customers on either side of the Atlantic. It's harder for entrepreneurs over here, he says, because buyers are naturally more sceptical about buying products from small firms and start-ups.

"In an entrepreneurial context, the biggest challenge between doing business here and the US is you get a lot more people rooting for your success in the US. There are a lot more ways that you can be visibly supported, not the least of which are more entrepreneurial customers."

Things are perhaps starting to change, especially with the popularity of the *Dragons' Den* programme that made Richard famous. But meanwhile start-ups need to anticipate this disadvantage and do all they can to instil confidence in their customers.

Don't obsess about the competition
Ian Powell, PricewaterhouseCoopers

PricewaterhouseCoopers is the number-one accountancy firm in the UK, so you would forgive its chairman, Ian Powell, for looking over his shoulder every now and then. But Powell says his company is not obsessed by its rivals and lately has, in fact, changed its focus to becoming an "iconic brand".

"Until recently we were overly interested in what our competitors did; it's one of the big things I've tried to change. We are the market leader and they should pick the paper up and say 'God, look what they've done now. We can't possibly top that'.

"We aren't ignoring our competitors, that would be naïve, but we have changed the game so that we worry about what we do and we look forward as a business and no longer worry about what the others are doing. We don't obsess about other firms, we'd rather they obsessed about us."

Make sure joint partnerships are legally binding
Kavita Oberoi, Oberoi Consulting

One way Kavita Oberoi chose to grow her business was through partnerships with other businesses operating in her market. While she maintains this is a great way to grow a small business, she cautions that firms must make arrangements official and legally binding.

"One way to grow is to form strategic alliances; when you're working with other companies in a similar field and you bring together two solutions that will make yours a little bit better. But it's really important to get your commercial agreements put in place very early.

"I had this fantastic idea, brought in a company, developed the market and when it was all ready they decided to run with it themselves. It makes you more aware of what can happen.

"If companies are turned off you because you're throwing legal stuff at them then you shouldn't be dealing with them in the first place. If they're a sound company they'd expect a formal and binding arrangement."

Get a good reputation early on
Mark Zaleski, DailyMotion

Good customer service could be the difference between entrepreneurial success and failure. When you start up a business, it's vital that you establish a good reputation with customers immediately. A poor track record early on could spell disaster for your business before it even gets going.

Mark Zaleski's experience as a senior manager with Federal Express reflects what can happen to a business when it gets things just right. In its case, timely deliveries and parcel tracking brought customers back time and again.

"Fed Ex was fixated on getting everything right so that it achieved 100% customer satisfaction. Worrying about the number of complaints you're getting is no fun at all. It's a lot more fun when it all works, the customers respect you and you can think about developing the business next week, next month and next year."

Find a market with no competitors
Simon Nixon, Moneysupermarket.com

Simon Nixon's most recent start-up, SimonEscapes, is a self-proclaimed low-risk venture set up to secure some of his capital in UK property – which he sees as a safe bet. Nixon says he chose high-end holiday property because it is a relatively untapped market.

Outside the UK, particularly in mainland Europe, expensive holiday lets are everywhere, but Nixon believes the growing trend for 'staycations' or 'holidays at home' means demand for luxury British holidays will increase. The lack of competition just makes the idea all the more enticing.

"We're not competing with anyone. We're testing the market with this concept and if we find that there's no market for this – though I'm pretty sure there is – we'll just end up with a collection of amazing properties in the best locations. They're going to enjoy capital appreciation over the next 20 years. I can go there myself and friends and family can visit. It's a low-risk venture."

Diversify your customer base

Steve Leach, Bigmouthmedia (marketing)

When the economy goes into a spin it is your customers that keep you going, according to Bigmouthmedia founder Steve Leach. So it's imperative you keep a healthy flow of custom from different sources. Negotiating new terms is one way to help them pay your bills, but to safeguard your business you need a broad customer base.

If one part of the economy – construction or manufacturing for example – is particularly hard hit in a recession, businesses serving and supplying that sector will inevitably come under pressure. But if those companies also serve other markets – say, retailers – the impact will be less.

"We have roughly 600 clients including 350 major brands and there's no particular reliance on any sector. We've got 18 airlines, seven hotel chains and 12 banks. It's part of a cyclical process; you can't grow at a phenomenal level indefinitely and you have to have periods of downtime where you consolidate and improve the infrastructure of your businesses. What helps you prevail is lots of financially stable, loyal customers."

Get out while the going is good
Syed Ahmed, *The Apprentice*

Before Syed Ahmed flirted with fame on TV show *The Apprentice*, he co-founded technology recruitment consultancy IT People. The company focused on an untapped niche within the market and early on the going was good, but soon the industry caught up and bigger companies muscled their way in.

Observing the changing marketplace and his business' increasingly tentative position within it, Ahmed sold his stake to his business partner and resigned as a director. He says being adaptable is a vital entrepreneurial trait, and that means knowing when it's time to call it quits.

"We grew really quickly initially. However, in the second year I started to doubt the niche we had in the market and I needed a new challenge – where there was some opportunity and not 10,000 people doing what we were doing. By the end of the year the market got flooded and five big agencies were working the accounts we were working on.

"They were putting ridiculously low rates in front of the client and doing deals to undercut the competition. They were monopolising the market and had huge revenue so could get away with it – it wasn't something we could deal with because the margins were so small."

Word of mouth beats all
Rob Shreeve, One Alfred Place

London business-club-founder Rob Shreeve says word-of-mouth marketing is the most valuable form of advertising there is. Endorsements from friends and colleagues are the main reason people make big buying decisions and Shreeve has found that members' recommendations are a major source of new clients.

"I walked though the lobby yesterday and heard someone say, 'what is this place?'. They hadn't heard of it, they'd come for a meeting and asked to be shown around. I see our members touring people round the club every day. About 70% of our members come from visits.

"You've got to keep up the visibility because word of mouth is crucial; even if someone doesn't need us they might know somebody else who does. 5-10% of members joined because of an article they read, but most joined because of word of mouth."

Use technology to level the playing field
Ajaz Ahmed, AKQA

As the head of a business creating online marketing, branding and functionality solutions for some of the world's most respected organisations, you'd expect Ajaz Ahmed to be a technology advocate. He believes it's possible for start-ups and small businesses to compete with multinational firms.

Technology means the cost of starting a business is much lower, and it is much easier and quicker for entrepreneurs to put together the essential ingredients. Communications are now cheaper, quicker and open to everyone, and Ahmed says this makes business accessible too.

"The most important thing about tech is how it levels the playing field, so it can help anyone with a good idea get to where they need to be. It's become much more of a meritocracy and I love that. The ease of accessing knowledge now is phenomenal – when I was growing up I'd have to go to a library to research a subject, whereas now I can access MIT's archives online."

FAMILY BUSINESSES

Business is in the blood
Adrian Moorhouse, Lane4

Adrian Moorhouse says being a businessman is in his DNA and believes the qualities that helped him win Olympic Gold – grit, determination and commitment – are the same family-bred characteristics that have propelled him to business success.

Moorhouse has no formal qualifications, but whilst growing up he was exposed to the mechanics of commerce through his father, a director at a wool-import business.

"My dad used to work from home a lot when I was a teenager and my brother and I would help him out with his books and sales calls. Business is intuitive. I didn't get a degree, let alone an MBA, and my father was the same, he left school at 14 and made his own way. I inherited that work ethic of 'go and get it'."

Treat family members like other employees
Charlie Mullins, Pimlico Plumbers

Pimlico Plumbers is in many ways a family-run business. One of Charlie Mullins' sons is a plumber, another is in charge of the command centre, his daughter works on the phones and his wife also has a hands-on role in the business. He jokes that if he had more family he'd be able to retire.

Mullins concludes that there is no downside to hiring family members, but it is worth noting that he does not lavish them with perks, nor does he give them preferential treatment. He believes his fairness is the reason the family set-up works.

"They don't slack off, I don't let them; and I don't give anything away unless I want to. The family who work for me, I genuinely believe, earn every penny. The reward they get is a good lifestyle, good houses, cars and holidays, just like anyone else I employ."

Make the most of family connections
Dame Mary Perkins, Specsavers

Dame Mary Perkins says being part of a family enterprise (even one with tens of thousands of staff) is a real bonus. She believes the benefits include a cohesive and like-minded management team, trust and an enhanced reputation with partners and suppliers.

"The main thing about having a family business is that the kids have started to think like me and my husband and we all know what each other is thinking before we say it. We get on very well, which is always an advantage, and they know what they like doing best so they're not ever competing with each other or getting in each other's way. All the staff really like it and so do our joint-venture partners."

Family is family; business is business
Deborah Meaden, *Dragons' Den*

Deborah Meaden first achieved notable entrepreneurial achievements with her parents' business Westst§ar holiday parks, a chain of campsites in the west of England. Starting at the bottom and rising through the ranks, Meaden eventually bought out her parents in a multi-million pound deal.

Critically, both sides treated it like any other transaction. Family ties were put aside and the process went through the normal stages of offer, negotiation and agreement. Meaden says this was the only way to get a satisfactory result, and to keep the family together through the experience.

"At the time I paid a pretty full price for that business; they wanted the highest price, I wanted the lowest price – that's how business works. We negotiated using a completely different set of advisers and it became very feisty. Luckily the family approach has always been 'business is business and family is family'.

"When you go through something like that it tests your relationship so I paid well for the business at the time. People might say in hindsight that it wasn't a lot of money; I can tell you it was for me. I had everything on the line."

Learn from your relations
Gerry Calabrese, The Hoxton Pony (bar)

It's handy to have an inspiring person in your family and although Gerry Calabrese has never gone into business with his father, world-famous mixologist Salvatore Calabrese, he draws inspiration from him on a daily basis.

Calabrese has followed his dad into the drinks industry and developed his skills as a mixologist and venue manager by appreciating Salvatore's skills behind the bar.

"My dad is my idol. He's one of the world's leading experts in vintage cognacs, and in 2009 he was voted number-one in the UK bar industry by the industry itself; he is a legend throughout the world.

"Me and my old man have a very good relationship; we talk daily and he's always offering me advice."

There is life outside the family firm
James Caan, *Dragons' Den*, Hamilton Bradshaw

James Caan was brought to the UK by his father when he was two years old. Settling in London's Brick Lane his father set up a business selling leather jackets. When Caan was a teenager he got his first job in recruitment and he later founded Alexander Mann, the recruitment chain that made his fortune.

Caan believes that having an entrepreneur as a parent was a motivating factor for a career in business, but he says it doesn't necessarily follow that entrepreneurs should join the family firm. His father initially disagreed, but when Caan launched his one hundredth global office his father conceded he was right.

"If you come from a family of actors it is quite likely you'll become an actor; if you come from a family where big brother or sister or mum or dad are doctors, the same is true. There is a pattern of people entering into the same environment as their relatives.

"In my case my father was an entrepreneur and I saw what it involved, experienced it and it did have an impact. I was inspired and motivated by it. I love the excitement and the freedom of being in a business where you are in control. I was turned on by risk, all or nothing – 'you don't succeed, you earn nothing'. I love the fear and the adrenaline caused by potentially having nothing."

Start a business when you're pregnant
Jennifer Irvine, The Pure Package

Jennifer Irvine has spent much of the past four years either pregnant or breast-feeding. Despite her growing brood, Irvine has also managed to grow The Pure Package, her health-food-delivery business, to £1m in sales annually.

She believes that pregnancy and maternity leave present the perfect opportunity to start thinking about or developing a business plan. Irvine herself confesses that she has a number of new ideas that occurred to her having founded her current business, but sadly she's keeping tight-lipped about them.

"I think that maternity leave could be a really great opportunity for somebody to start a business. Six months is plenty of time. It can be a wonderful opportunity, especially after your first child.

"When your life gets jigged around you recognise opportunities you wouldn't see normally. It's a chance to suddenly have new ideas. Now I'm coming up with loads of business ideas for mothers – there are lots of exciting things you can do once you start up in business."

For success in business, get married
Mark Constantine, Lush

Lush founder Mark Constantine's main piece of advice to fledgling entrepreneurs is to "marry well". He reckons a supportive spouse is the bedrock of any successful start-up and the more involved they are in the business the better.

"You need lots of support as an entrepreneur and my wife is actively involved in the business. We have a lovely time together and I think that makes a big difference. If you don't have any relationship at all then you're probably building an unbalanced life for yourself, which isn't good for you.

"We are fortunate, a lot of people at the top of our business are very happily married and that gives it a great deal of stability because there's not too much philandering or messing about and you can focus on what you're meant to focus on.

"When we used to meet potential partners, my colleague would bring his children along to see how irritated they were by the kids. If they were very irritated by it then you wouldn't do business with them."

You don't have to hand it on
Rupert Clevely, Geronimo Inns

It is important to know your goals in business, according to Rupert Clevely, founder of Geronimo Inns, and that means being honest with yourself about your true aspirations. To hand a successful business down through the generations is a noble ambition, but it's fine to build a short-term venture for profit too.

"I don't tend to see this as a long-term plan for the Clevelys. I don't want to be here for the next 20 years. I'm not going to pass this down to my daughters. I want to make some money out of it and then I want to relax a bit more because I left school at 17 and have been working every day since then, so that's quite important to me."

Family and business fit perfectly
Sarah Beeny, *Property Ladder*, Tepilo.com

Sarah Beeny thinks that family and business go together well. Her father was a big influence on her development as an entrepreneur and she has involved her husband in all of her ventures. She even thinks pregnancy is a good time to start a business.

"I have a theory that when you're pregnant that's when you should do all the work; it's after you've had the baby that you want to do nothing. I have three children already so I made a rod for my own back.

"I was terribly bad at school and my father would cut out press articles about entrepreneurs and go 'Oh, look at this'. He never wanted me to work in a city; instead he would always go on about Anita Roddick and Richard Branson. He would point to things that they did and say 'you could do this too'. They were the kind of people who were waved in front of me at every possible opportunity.

"When I got a bad grade he would say, 'Never mind, look at what Richard Branson has done!' He gave me the confidence to say, 'Yeah, I can do that'. It's all about confidence.

"My father was an architect and we were around building sites all the time. So I know buildings quite well. All of our businesses are to do with family and home."

A loving family is the keystone of any entrepreneur
Sir Tom Farmer, Kwik-Fit

For Sir Tom Farmer, the support of those closest to you is vital in developing the confidence to start and run a successful business. Farmer acknowledges his luck at having a supportive family and community growing up as a child and similarly accommodating managers in his first job.

The feeling of security he got from his comfortable early years gave Farmer the grounding to set up his chain of tyre depots, which eventually grew into Kwik-Fit.

"We all enjoyed the success that we shared in, but also there were people to encourage and inspire me to get up and carry on when I stumbled and made mistakes. Sometimes things don't work out and if you're on your own you can just fall into despair.

"Mine is not a rags-to-riches story because we were surrounded by people who cared and shared; the people in the street, police, nuns in the church or teachers, we were just surrounded by it.

"When I talk to my brothers and sisters about it, we talk about our mum and dad who were the best in the world, but also that tremendous feeling of security; knowing you're surrounded by people who'd always help you when you needed support."

Unless you start together, keep business and family separate

Rob Shreeve, One Alfred Place

The jury seems to be out on doing business with close friends and relatives. Rob Shreeve of One Alfred Place business club says his past experiences have been on the whole less than positive. Unless entering into business as 50:50 shareholders at the start, it's best not to mix business and family, he says.

"I think on the whole I wouldn't recommend doing business with friends because it complicates the relationship. One of my oldest friends invested in the business and because of our friendship wanted to be more involved than was possible and it hasn't helped our friendship. On the other hand, I do recommend having investors that you know and like.

"Life's too short to take money for the sake of it. There's too much time wasted on politics if you're working with people who are fighting each other all the time. But I think there's a line you shouldn't cross, which is very close friends, and partners even."

LUCK

Luck is a factor but hard work makes the difference

Adrian Moorhouse, Lane4

Adrian Moorhouse was brought up to not believe in luck, but he acknowledges that it plays its part in business. While hard work and competence will get you far, most successful entrepreneurs have experienced some form of fortune in their career. For Moorhouse it was meeting his co-founders.

"I met my co-founders at Loughborough University. They had been commissioned by 3M to train their managers like coaches train athletes; they had taken a chance because they thought it would be useful.

"I was working for the Olympics Association at the time and I happened to share a room with one of the guys. I saw that the idea had legs and that these academics were undercharging for the service, so I said, 'Let's start a business'. It stemmed from that chance encounter."

Take advantage of your circumstances

Dame Mary Perkins, Specsavers

Dame Mary Perkins admits she has experienced her fair share of luck in business. Her choice of profession, the period in which she started her business and the fact that she met her husband when she did all contributed to the stellar success of the Specsavers brand.

"We've definitely been lucky; lucky that I'm an optometrist, lucky that I met my husband at university and he thinks the same as I do, and lucky for the time that we started up. It was when Margaret Thatcher was in power and, although taxes were high, it was a time when there wasn't the red tape around that there is now.

"When we first got going we also benefitted from deregulation in the market, which gave us a freer hand to advertise our products and services. Today, advertising is one of our big differentiators and the ability to shout about what we do has helped enormously."

Make the best of a bad situation
David Gold, Ann Summers

David Gold says luck comes in a number of different forms and good luck can sometimes be disguised as bad, depending on how you react to it. He believes that a stroke of 'bad luck' when he was a fledgling businessman propelled him to become the retail magnate he is today.

"I could demonstrate a number of times when I've cursed my luck. I was running my little bookshop on Charing Cross Road and had been at it for three years; my fortunes had turned for the better. Then suddenly the landlord told me my lease was up and I had to get out.

"Because of that bad luck, I took the money I had made and put deposits on four stores. Two of them I've still got to this day and they are valued at £10m. More importantly, however, the other two I bought for £20,000 each and ten years later I sold them for £3m – and that was when £3m was a lot of money!"

Never look a gift horse in the mouth
Kanya King, MOBO Awards

Kanya King wasn't the first to have the idea for an event celebrating music of black origin. Many had tried and failed before her. Although there are plenty of reasons why King succeeded, she admits a chance encounter with a senior television executive led to a huge boost for her start-up business.

"In the beginning I'd be talking to people about the MOBO awards and nobody had heard of it. They didn't understand it. We launched the concept at the Ministry of Sound and generated a lot of interest and a lot of media coverage.

"Then, at Arsenal's football ground, I happened to bump into a gentleman who I didn't know at the time was managing director of LWT. He was looking for his son and I helped him out. Afterwards we got talking and I said, 'I've got a great idea' – that's probably what everyone says to him – and I told him about the concept.

"Lo and behold, I sent in a proposal and they called me in for a meeting. We showed them all the coverage generated at the launch and the plans that we had and they thought it was fantastic."

Be in the right place at the right time
Max Clifford, PR

Even business greats like Max Clifford need a bit of luck from time to time. Clifford admits he was fortunate to enter PR just as it was developing as an industry. Having cut his teeth in record label EMI's press office during the 1960s, he had access to up and coming new acts who became the first clients of his start-up business.

"Because I was at the right time and place, I had a good working knowledge of the industry and what went on, so it gradually took off. I never had a plan, one door opened and then another one opened."

Luck is not the same as effort
Michelle Dewberry, *The Apprentice*, Chiconomise

Michelle Dewberry once incurred the wrath of a successful person by innocently suggesting they were 'lucky'. It taught her two valuable lessons; the first is that most wealthy people are hard workers; the second is that you shouldn't call a hard worker lucky.

"I was once at a very famous and wealthy lady's house, which is very beautiful, and I remember telling her she was so lucky, considering where she lives. She said, 'Don't you ever say that', and really lost her temper saying, 'Everything in my life I've earned'.

"You've got to create your own luck. You can't just sit in your house and wait for a lucky break, you've got to make it happen."

It's good to start-up in an evolving market
Sir Tom Farmer, Kwik-Fit

Sir Tom Farmer had the good fortune of starting his tyre retail business just as rules affecting the sale of goods were changing in his favour. In the 1960s the practice of discounting on manufactured goods was legitimised and Farmer was one of the first to slash his prices.

The new wave of discount shops drew interest from the press and as one of the first to make his move Farmer landed an interview with a major local paper. The response from customers who read the article was overwhelmingly positive and Farmer has never looked back.

"The law was just changing so discounters were popping up all over the place. I opened up a shop in Edinburgh. It was £5 rent, £5 to my mother for housekeeping and £5 to go out at the weekend. One of the newspapers decided to write an article about me. "I think I exaggerated slightly because they asked me about who my suppliers were; they could still get into trouble at that stage so I told them how I get in my van in the middle of the night and meet people in dark lay-bys. I never thought too much about it afterwards.

"A couple of weeks later one of the Sunday papers came in and the headline in the front page had my name on it. I always go to Mass on a Sunday, I'd have a quick cup of coffee and go and open the shop for 11am. That particular Sunday there were 42 cars outside. It never stopped from that moment."

LEADERSHIP

Don't worry about the things you can't change
Ian Powell, PricewaterhouseCoopers

As chairman and senior partner of PricewaterhouseCoopers with responsibility for a group of countries housing 77,000 PwC staff, Ian Powell could be forgiven for having the odd sleepless night. Stress is a problem for high-powered corporate executives and entrepreneurs alike.

But when Powell feels a touch of anxiety coming on he remembers a blood pressure-lowering anecdote featuring former Reuters chairman and personal hero of Powell's, Sir Christopher Hogg.

"I saw Sir Christopher Hogg at a seminar. His great mentor was [former GEC chairman] Arnie Weinstock. He once asked Hogg, 'What keeps you awake at night?'. Hogg replied, 'Exchange rates, the local economy, interest rates'. Weinstock says 'So what are you going to do about them?'. 'Nothing. I can't,' says Hogg. 'So why worry?' Weinstock shoots back.

"The moral of the story is, worry about the things you can affect. There's not a lot you can do about the environment you work in but there's lots you can change in your own environment. We've been a very conservative organisation in a very conservative industry, but that is changing."

Share your plans with employees
Gil Steyaert, Adidas

As one of sportswear giant Adidas' most senior managing directors, Gil Steyaert must give direction and clarity to thousands of employees throughout Europe. He has years of experience in managing big teams and he believes many of his lessons are relevant to small business owners too.

Steyaert believes the best way to mobilise staff is to provide them with a vision. A set of goals three or five years in the future gives your team an overarching sense of purpose. For Adidas it is the Olympic Games, for which it is a primary sponsor, but for small firms it could be new products, expansion targets or financial goals.

"A three or five-year plan is very important because businesses that don't have one are navigating in the fog. You have to build something to generate growth, so create a galvanising vision. It will create clarity of purpose, and a mantra that people can grasp and look to for inspiration. Clarify the company purpose and inspire the staff."

Don't try to do it yourself
James Caan, *Dragons' Den*, Hamilton Bradshaw

No one is good at everything, not even multi-millionaire entrepreneurs. When you start in business it's likely you'll have several roles to fulfil, including marketing, accounting and sales. But as you grow it will become more important to fill these roles with expert recruits.

James Caan is no exception. He admits he has an unusually large number of employees for a private equity firm, but that his specialists can complete tasks that would flummox him. It means the company is efficient and professional and can offer investees more than just money.

"I'm invested in 40 businesses and I'm heavily involved with them all. I'm very fortunate to have a team of 22 people. Not every business needs me every day although I do work seven days a week. In the vast majority of cases, issues that arise in business are taken care of by the specialists I have in my team.

"I structured the business so that if in the next three months I think that the main problem facing us is a particular issue, my natural reaction would be to hire someone to fill that need. I'm a generalist, I understand about entrepreneurship but I couldn't deal with a tax problem or an IT problem or an HR issue."

If you feel stressed, make a list
Jennifer Irvine, The Pure Package

Jennifer Irvine thinks the hardest thing about running a business is getting the work/life balance right. All entrepreneurs experience stress at some point in their careers and for many it is an ever-present feature of running a business. It needn't ruin the experience, however, and Irvine has a few tricks for lowering her blood pressure.

"The hardest thing about business is balance. Some days I think I've got it absolutely right and other days I just think, 'What have I done?'. When that happens I sit on the loo and think it out. I have a notebook and I write down any frustrations I have, so that it doesn't become too claustrophobic for me.

"It can be quite overwhelming with the number of things that are going on. I'm a real list-maker. I scribble down any issues that I have and then I deal with them. Once I've written them down, the stress generally goes away magically, because then I know I won't forget the issues. It's a bit boring but it works for me."

Keep your team together
Kanya King, MOBO Awards

Kanya King's dream of creating a huge music event dedicated to black artists seemed like a colossal undertaking for her start-up team and a few concluded that the jump from kitchen table to world stage was too great. King's toughest challenge in the early days was to keep believing and prevent the team from giving up.

"When I started I had some great friends, but when people aren't getting paid for it, they would make up excuses when I called meetings. It was frustrating. I remember we were sitting around a friend's kitchen table and we were all coming up with ideas and concepts and it was all very exciting.

"We arranged to meet again the following week, but then people dropped by the wayside and it was difficult. You try to keep people on board but at the same time they've got to make money and it's not as easy for them because it's your vision and your dream. People also have to consider the chances of it working."

Know when to let go of responsibilities
Kavita Oberoi, Oberoi Consulting

For healthcare consultancy entrepreneur Kavita Oberoi, the hardest part of running a business is letting go of your responsibilities. As a business grows, its founders put more and more trust in employees to take care of mounting workloads – a fact that many entrepreneurs find hard to accept.

"What I found stressful and what I still find stressful today – and this is what every entrepreneur will find difficult – is getting results through other people, because as an entrepreneur you think that only you can deliver. It's relinquishing that control.

"So if somebody else takes over your worry, are they going to deliver results that are up to your standard? I found that really difficult. Over the last few years I've set up performance-management systems and standards and that probably should have been done right at the start, but a lot of entrepreneurs just have everything in their head."

Pick investors that will let you lead
Keith Potts, Jobsite

When Jobsite.co.uk was sold to the Daily Mail group (DMGT), its co-founder Keith Potts wanted to make sure he would still have incentives to develop the business further. The deal left him with a stake in the business and performance-related bonuses, but Potts says the most important aspect of the deal was that the buyers left him with a feeling that he still runs the show.

To other entrepreneurs planning to sell their business but stay on as a senior manager, he recommends picking investors who adopt a relaxed approach and allow you to run the business with a free hand.

"We were left with a stake in the company. The problem arises when you come to the end of an earn-out; what do you do then? They're very clever at incentivising you going forward. I'm now coming up for my third earn-out. The way it's structured, I still pretty much feel that it's our business."

To be a great leader, you must believe in yourself
Lord Bilimoria, Cobra Beer

Lord Bilimoria's father was the Indian equivalent of a four-star general and when he retired was in charge of 350,000 soldiers. Bilimoria junior couldn't help picking up management advice with such a responsible role model in the house. He uses many of his father's managerial traits in his own business.

"I observed my father at first hand over the years and always saw the way in which he dealt with people. I saw the way he delegated and his principle of having not just an efficient team but a happy team. I also witnessed his cool, calm and collectedness in a crisis situation.

"There is no single template of a perfect leader, or a charismatic, inspirational leader; everyone is different, each leadership style is different. But what makes leadership effective is that you are a truly authentic leader and that you're true to your own beliefs.

"This is something that I've inherited from my father: there is nothing on my desk apart from the thing I'm working on now. I never used to be like that, papers used to be piled up; but he said no, you've got to have a clean desk. I do have papers stacked, but in an orderly way in which I can access them when I need them. In front of me is clean."

Align your 'honesty lines'
Mark Zaleski, DailyMotion

Silicon Valley whiz-kid Mark Zaleski argues that the people you start a business with are vitally important. They should be determined, passionate and skilful, certainly, but equally important is that founders share the same moral code. As he puts it, people's 'honesty lines' should be properly aligned.

"It comes down to liking the people you work with and having the same values. You must surround yourself with the same values but different skill sets. Choose people who are good at what they do, but care about how they get there because the end doesn't justify the means.

"Lots of people justify their actions in their heads, but you must make sure that everyone's honesty lines are the same. You can't have people who fudge things, you want to know that the ones in the fox hole with you are all on the same side looking out for each other.

"I'd rather do something that was less exiting and more limiting but with the right people, because you are more likely to have a good time and be more successful – then you won't have to look back with regret."

Make sure your business can do without you
Martha Lane Fox, Lastminute.com

Martha Lane Fox left Lastminute.com in 2003, after the business had recovered from the dotcom fallout and achieved profitability. Lane Fox said she always wanted to duck out on a high and made certain the business would be unaffected by her departure.

"It's much worse to leave a business if it's not going well and I wanted to leave mine when it was going brilliantly. I always said I wanted to bow out when we reached profitability and that's what I did.

"It wasn't a surprise to Brent [Hoberman]. I loved the business but it's the mark of a good business if it's not reliant on any one person. I felt proud that I could walk out of the door and it would have no real impact on the business at all. All they would say is, 'That girl is missing from the building'."

If you want freedom, don't take investment
Michelle Dewberry, *The Apprentice*, Chiconomise

Investors can be a bit like bosses, according to *The Apprentice* winner Michelle Dewberry, so be wary of taking on investment unnecessarily; especially if your goal as an entrepreneur is freedom. Dewberry was offered various amounts when she started Chiconomise.com, but turned them all down.

"I wanted Chiconomise to be a proven concept and to grow organically. Getting investors involved on day one is almost a bit unnecessary. If you're a good business person you should be able to make stuff happen on a budget without it looking like it's on a budget.

"You have to ask: what are they actually bringing? I started my business because I want to be free. I don't want a meeting on a Friday with someone saying 'You were supposed to grow your subscriber base by 100 today and you only managed 50' – that's not much fun."

Get structured or lose direction
Rupert Clevely, Geronimo Inns

The stereotype entrepreneur is a risk-happy chancer who seeks out opportunities without giving much thought to the consequences. But as a business grows, employing staff and developing product lines, the scope for risk-taking shrinks.

For Rupert Clevely, business owners – however entrepreneurial – must introduce an element of structure to the business. He believes formal processes and dependable protocols stabilise businesses as they grow; business owners that don't adjust are a lot more likely to come a cropper, he says.

"The danger is that the bigger you get, the less entrepreneurial you become, because you have to naturally become more structured. But structure is no bad thing for an entrepreneur.

"I think that's where businesses fail, when they don't have structure. The best blend is an entrepreneur with lots of flair and ideas, who's also got the ability to understand that they've got to have structure. If they don't have structure it's simply not going to work."

Know your strengths as a leader
Sam Malin, Madagascar Oil

Madagascar Oil founder Sam Malin says his strengths lie in starting businesses, not growing them into multinational concerns. Having founded the company, he sought partners and investment and started the process of proving that his wells had economically viable reserves of oil.

Once the project was established and had grown into a large business, Malin stepped back from executive duties, allowing a team of professional managers to take over the running of the company. He advises other entrepreneurs to identify their strengths and weaknesses and to recruit people who can fill the gaps.

"My strength is to identify and originate projects, get the initial investment in, promote the projects and get them up and running, but it's probably not running a large, sophisticated company.

"I would rather start something new. There are entrepreneurial managers of big companies but if I had stayed on I would have needed lots of people around me to fill in that professional part and I wouldn't have had time to work on new ideas.

"Being a professional manager is not what I most like to do; I like getting the project up, running and financed. That said, my new company, Avana Petroleum, is a little different because of my experience in the oil industry. I've learned a lot from Madagascar Oil."

Keep yourself healthy if you want to lead
Simon Nixon, Moneysupermarket.com

One of Simon Nixon's fundamental business rules is to keep your body in decent nick. Running a business – whether it succeeds or fails – can be an exhausting experience, and you'll need energy to get over the inevitable bumps in the road.

"Make sure you stay fit and healthy. That's very important. So I eat healthily, I work out, do lots of yoga and I have reflexology to keep myself in tip-top condition. You need lots and lots of energy and drive, because if you haven't got that and belief in what you're doing, you're going to fail."

You don't have to be in London to build a big business

Steve Leach, Bigmouthmedia

Many big companies have headquarters in major cities. But apart from the bright lights, growing businesses don't miss out on much by locating in smaller cities and towns.

In Britain, the traditional home of successful businesses are the big powerhouse cities, but Steve Leach, founder of Bigmouthmedia, has chosen the less obvious towns of Edinburgh, Munich and Trondheim in Norway from which to run his empire.

"Those places don't seem the best places to start a global business but there are very good smart people, including good calibre graduates, around Edinburgh that we picked up in the early days. There's less churn because there are fewer competitors to poach our staff and, I would argue, a better standard of living.

"Plus everything is just that little bit cheaper, which allows us to be competitive and more stable when the market has really been nuts."

Act differently

Wayne Hemingway, Red or Dead

Red or Dead was the ultimate non-conformist fashion label. Co-founders Wayne and Gerardine Hemingway steered clear of the normal PR-hungry champagne-sloshing socialites and celebrity catwalk events; and developed a reputation in the media as a result.

Doing something different can help a business grow, according to Wayne, because it creates an individual identity for the brand and sets it apart in a crowded marketplace.

"We were different because we didn't go to all the dos or take our kids to catwalk shows (the sorts of things that happen in the fashion industry). Husband-and-wife teams were just a strange thing for the industry. The fact I wanted to talk about football and didn't want anything to do with celebrity was also unusual.

"That helped us with the public, or at least the section of the public that understood what we stood for. If we wanted to become part of the establishment in the fashion industry and get that kind of publicity then it hindered us, but we wanted to do it another way. We stayed underground and the people who agreed with us got to know us.

"Red or Dead was a very political company in terms of its sloganeering, what it stood up for and its support of the environment, and all our jeans were made in a full-security prison in York by lifers. That meant retraining them, which worked as a story.

"We were the first to make denim out of cannabis resin. So that was a great story too, because all of our jeans were made using hemp, by lifers, in a maximum-security prison. And we knew what we were doing, because there was a little message behind it all. We were very clever, because what a story that made."

React quickly when things go wrong
Dawn Gibbins, Flowcrete

Even fast-growing successful businesses can get into trouble financially. When they do it is down to management to uncover the cause and eliminate it. In the case of Flowcrete, the manufacturing business run by Dawn Gibbins, trouble came when the company grew to £20m turnover and developed 100 products.

Gibbins identified several problems, including the fact that she had taken her eye off the ball after winning a major entrepreneurial award. The business had grown too complex and communication was at an all-time low. Responding quickly, Gibbins turned a loss into a large profit in two years through what she calls a 'corporate detox'.

"We looked at why we weren't bringing the sales in and it boiled down to three key reasons: the communication in our company was crap –

nobody knew where we were going; we were too complicated; and we weren't training people enough."

Quick and thoughtful measures – streamlining the product range and introducing incentive schemes – were introduced to solve it.

Don't use technology for technology's sake
Charlie Mullins, Pimlico Plumbers

A plumber by training and with no academic credentials to speak of, Charlie Mullins has built up a multi-million pound business without the use of a computer. He concedes he wouldn't be able to turn one on, but argues that people too often hide behind the technology.

"The thing about computers is they can't answer yes or no and my business is run on yes or no. People rely too much on computers; I get people coming into work and they say, 'My computer's not working so I can't do anything'. I say, 'You can talk can't you?'.

"I'm on the phone all the time, including on my way into work, but I don't need it to sing and dance, I just want it to ring and for me to be able to have a conversation on it. Everything else is really just a distraction for me. Most of my calls are a few seconds long; we talk, make a decision then hang up."

MARKETING AND PR

Marketing starts at home
Gerry Calabrese, The Hoxton Pony

Gerry Calabrese has invested a lot of time and effort on PR and marketing for his bar, The Hoxton Pony. But, he says, fundamentally, marketing starts with the bar itself, which is after all the bit that his customers are guaranteed to see. His mission is to stand out in an area littered with bars, and he achieves it.

"The whole idea was to do something different for Shoreditch. We didn't want to have the same tired theme that's been running round here since the 1990s. I've lived and worked here for the last eight years. It's the same old exposed bricks and battered Chesterfields, the tables that your arms stick to and terrible service.

"We do quarterly marketing plans, just because the fashions and trends change so quickly and you've got different places opening up all the time. I like to review everything to make sure that we know the new trends, the new music and to be aware of what's happening. It's very important to keep one step ahead."

Social networking sites are great marketing tools
Michelle Dewberry, *The Apprentice*, Chiconomise

Michelle Dewberry is now a dotcom entrepreneur and as such is a backer of all things online. She is particularly enamoured with Twitter, the micro-blogging website allowing users to broadcast short messages and links to their 'followers'.

Dewberry thinks it's a great free marketing tool and uses it to bring traffic to her money-saving website for girls, Chiconomise.com. The trick, she says, is give people an incentive to visit her website with tempting offers, deals and competitions.

"I've just bought a new domain called TwitStop.com and I'm working out exactly what to do with that. I mentioned it on Twitter and said I wanted to do something fun; the best idea wins a prize. I think it's an incredibly powerful vehicle. But I admit that to the untrained eye it can look ridiculous.

"On my website, apart from Google, Twitter is the biggest referring site. We put deals on there. We're in the process of acquiring some competition prizes to give people an incentive to follow us.

"Following someone on Twitter is unobtrusive, whereas when you sign up to a website it can be intrusive. There are also applications like TweetDeck, where you can put your best friends in a column; you can just look at what you want to look at and ignore the rest. I'm a massive advocate."

Use every advantage, but stay on message
Adrian Moorhouse, Lane4

Adrian Moorhouse has a unique advantage when it comes to promoting his business. As a famous former Olympic gold medallist he is guaranteed press coverage when he needs it, but for Moorhouse it's a double-edged sword. Coverage is not always on message and he often finds himself answering questions about sport, not business.

"The first publicity we get must be about the business. There have been lots of opportunities to do PR-friendly stuff, such as working with the British Lions, but I didn't want to get anywhere near that because I wanted our work to speak for itself.

"The PR has got to be on message, otherwise there's a danger we'll head down the ex-sportsperson motivational-talking-company route instead of a really strong HR consultancy that is competing against Deloitte and KPMG – that's where I want to be.

"The double-edged sword with PR is the more I get press the more people say 'Oh, it's that ex-swimmer', rather than 'There's that great business leader'. I don't think I'll ever be known as that because the swimming thing always comes first."

Don't try to cheat search engines
Steve Leach, Bigmouthmedia

One of the biggest mistakes businesses make online is trying to 'cheat' search engines into sending traffic their way. As the founder of a company that builds brands online, Steve Leach is acutely aware of this. His firm takes a responsible position when it comes to getting found on Google.

"I've heard of occasions where Google has banned websites. They will nearly always send an email to say something that you are doing is prohibited and they list what it is. If you don't stop then they take action, which is fair enough really, as they publish guidelines. A good example of a Google no-no is buying links to make sites look more popular than they are.

"We spend a lot of money with Google and have a close relationship with them. We get some clients coming to us saying, 'We're spending £10,000 a month with you and these crappy guys are ahead of us!', and we say it's because what they're doing is unethical. Sometimes it takes months before Google catches up, but sites do get penalised."

Communicate on the customer's terms
Ajaz Ahmed, AKQA

Working in a high-technology environment where jargon is commonplace, Ajaz Ahmed works hard to ensure that AKQA communicates with clients in plain English. The goal is to help clients understand problems and solutions, so they feel comfortable with the work being done. Baffling them with techno speak won't win you respect, he says.

"We were and are enthusiasts about digital technology; when you have that you want to share it with others. We see AKQA as a mechanism to share our love for technology. We wanted to demystify it and take away some of the voodoo for the great people we work for.

"Our clients have always respected that. To this day we don't use buzzwords, we use straightforward language. That goes a long way because our job is so much about accessibility as well as creating something that impresses. When people understand you clearly, they can share in your passion."

Take the right people out to lunch
Brad Burton, 4Networking

When Brad Burton had a stint as a computer-games journalist during the 1990s, he was struck by the PR industry's attitude to winning friends in editorial departments: what surprised him was that they wined and dined the editors, not the staff writers who produced the copy.

"PRs used to come in and take the editor out for lunch, and I used to think 'you idiots', because they were never the ones who wrote the piece. Today's staff writer is tomorrow's assistant editor. I think that's where I got the benchmark for treating everyone equally."

Take every opportunity that comes your way
Charlie Mullins, Pimlico Plumbers

Charlie Mullins' Pimlico Plumbers makes full use of PR opportunities to spread its brand. Mullins himself has made a string of TV appearances, including as part of a panel criticising MPs expenses and as an undercover worker on *The Secret Millionaire*.

His part-time staff member Buster Martin, aged 102, regularly hits the headlines for undertaking acts that defy his advanced years, including completing a couple of London marathons. Meanwhile, the firm's official band made it to the latter stages of a popular TV talent competition.

"The celebrity thing is serious business. A lot of our client base is celebrities; once you work for one they recommend you to another. There's not a week that goes by where we don't get on TV or radio. It's unusual if we don't land something to do with PR. There's no harm in promoting a good product.

"We do our PR through Max Clifford and he is the best in the business in my view. His celebrity contacts are unbelievable and he knows how to get the best out of his client base. I couldn't name another publicist to be honest, so he was an obvious choice for us."

Do-it-yourself marketing
Craig Sams, Green & Black's

Green & Black's is one of Britain's best-loved and trusted brands, yet the name was the product of a 15-minute brainstorming session by founders Craig Sams and Josephine Fairley. It goes to show that a bit of heartfelt consideration can produce an outcome every bit as good as the best creative agencies.

"As far as choosing the name was concerned, it was simple brainstorming. We sat around a table and it was Josephine who came up with it. We started with obvious, worthy names like Eco-choc that didn't sound very appetising.

"Once we had decided to go with a traditional Callard & Bowser-type name, Green & Black's immediately leapt to the top. And once we had it that was it, no more discussion. We knew we weren't going to get any better. It was a very quick process – in all, perhaps 15 minutes."

Awards are great for your brand
Jennifer Irvine, The Pure Package

Jennifer Irvine has picked up a trophy cabinet full of awards for her entrepreneurial achievements but Irvine says awards are not an end in themselves; they are a useful tool for promoting the business and giving it a seal of quality.

"Winning awards is not a goal of mine. It's good because it validates the company. When you win something like *Harper's Bazaar* Entrepreneur of the Year, you've got a big magazine saying, 'You are the best'. I won a BT Essence of the Entrepreneur Award. When you win that, you're able to attach yourself to the brand.

"BT is saying that I'm real. Companies like that add validation to your brand, and now I've got people buying food three months in advance. Recently someone bought food for himself and his whole entourage and paid for five months in advance. It's great that I've got all these awards because you wouldn't just write a cheque to Joe Bloggs for £10,000."

Your brand is important, so protect it
Kanya King, MOBO Awards

Kanya King has worked hard to build the MOBO Organisation into an international brand without detracting from its urban roots. She achieved this by rejecting offers from companies that would make them money but risk them being deemed a sell-out.

Instead, King used the MOBO brand to help not-for-profit groups and charities. And, although recently MOBO has linked up with more private companies on profit-making ventures, she has been careful to pair with firms that reflect the organisation's founding principles.

"In a lot of ways the brand is untapped, so we've spent over a decade with a strong marketing policy that ultimately allows us to extend the brand into other products and services. Some of the things we're doing now, and the people that are contacting us, have helped us to build and diversify into other areas.

"Fantastic companies are contacting us to do books, to do shows and events and that's the reach of the brand; there are so many areas where we can extend. For example, we've had a fashion company approach us and they want to design a limited-edition merchandise range."

Be an innovative marketer
Keith Potts, Jobsite

Jobsite spends millions of pounds a year on marketing and PR but even before they developed a huge war chest, co-founder Keith Potts and his team were coming up with innovative ways to spread the brand across the internet.

"All the time we were thinking of the next big thing. We did a viral game one Christmas. It was at a time when flash was just coming out and people didn't really know what to do with it. We did a reindeer racing game where you could race your mates.

"The MD of a competitor rang me up saying, 'You've got all my staff playing your game!'. I remember at the time of the '97 elections we did a make-your-own movie of the politicians of the day. We did viral campaigns when people hadn't really heard of viral and millions of people downloaded them."

Bridge the credibility gap
Lord Bilimoria, Cobra Beer

Lord Bilimoria believes brand building starts the moment you launch your business. But when you're an unknown it is your personal brand that dictates whether your business will be taken seriously. He argues that passion and confidence are two qualities that kick-start businesses.

"The hardest thing about getting your brand off the ground is bridging the credibility gap, because you start with nothing and nobody knows you or your brand. Why do people supply you, why do they finance you, why do they buy from you? The single reason they do is if you have complete faith, passion, belief, and confidence in your product and in yourself.

"That gives people the confidence to trust you and to give you a chance. That's your starting point, then you've got to convince your customers to buy. You go through those phases and eventually your plane should take off. Stick with it."

It's okay to gamble with your brand
Mark Constantine, Lush

Mark Constantine's successful Lush chain is famously conscientious. Part of the reputation comes from its many donations to charities supporting various good causes. But Lush also tempts controversy by backing unloved direct-action movements such as Plane Stupid.

Constantine is unapologetic about this decision and says it is yet to have a negative impact on sales. He believes most people sympathise with the basic point of direct-action groups and this is why Lush's turnover has continued to grow.

"It depends on the individual, where you stand and whether you think this is a good thing or a bad thing. But they are our principals and it becomes difficult for us to swap them round to suit others. If it had too much of a negative impact on sales then we wouldn't we able to give the money, would we?

"Sadly, in the end, if you like our charities then that's lovely and we really appreciate your support. If you don't, well I'm sorry, but that's who we are and when you buy from us you are buying from those individuals and that is the truth of the matter."

Marketing is not a uniform discipline
Mark Zaleski, DailyMotion

While working at Federal Express early in his career, Mark Zaleski was struck by the varying attitudes to advertising held by Fed Ex customers in different countries. It's worth noting for growing businesses that a marketing strategy that works wonders in the UK could fail elsewhere in the world.

"There's less floweriness in America, even in the language, and customers expect to get at least what they pay for. It's changed in the last 20 years – the US has softened very slightly and is perhaps a bit more polished, and in the UK we're a bit more direct. But there are still obvious differences.

"Culturally I think shouting about yourself would put Brits off, we like to support the underdog, but, saying that, these days we want things to work as well. We're used to proper customer service and getting the service we've paid for. With globalisation it's more acceptable to say 'We're the best'."

Understand the media and what you want from it
Max Clifford, PR

Max Clifford says the key to marketing is to understand the media and the behaviour of publications you want to target, as well as the journalists that work for them. Just as important is understanding what you want to achieve through a PR campaign. Clifford's business is often about suppressing news.

"It's important to recognise the power of the media and to get as much control as possible. That's all you can do, try to understand the way it works, the people and the way to get the best for your particular client – for me it's more often about what you stop than what you start."

Get on TV
Peter Jones, *Dragons' Den*, Phones International

Dragons' Den's Peter Jones was a noteworthy entrepreneur with a multi-million pound fortune before he appeared on the hit TV show, but he admits that being in front of a camera pushed him to new heights in business.

Even the contestants on *Dragons' Den* who refuse or are turned down for investment often go on to do fantastically well due to the huge PR value of the show. If you can get your business in front of a TV audience, it's bound to prosper, says Jones.

"*Dragons' Den* is something that occurred completely out of the blue. It has just evolved. There are positives and negatives working in television but it certainly opens doors in business; people are more interested to meet me or one of my group-companies than they would have been before.

"I think there is a kudos element there that works for us and I think it's important that people want to follow in the footsteps of entrepreneurs who are in the public eye. I think that's a great thing for business in this country."

Understand how your business affects others
Sam Malin, Madagascar Oil

As the founder of a business in the energy and minerals-extraction industries, Sam Malin is more sensitive than most to the public's perception of his company. His businesses have an environmental, economic and sociological impact and one of his responsibilities is to ensure that this effect is positive overall.

He has taken steps to mitigate the harmful side-effects of mining, as well as the potential for disease cross-infection between groups of migrant workers, and to balance the sensitivities of an environmentally conscious world with the demands of a large African island that wants to develop.

"It's unavoidable that a mining project will have a negative impact on the environment, at least in the local area, so the key is to make sure there is also a positive impact.

"We work with the Malagasy ministry of the environment, local and international NGOs. For example, there is one very well-known group that is working with us on a coal project; coal is seen in a bad light in Europe, but in Madagascar 86% of energy is generated by burning the existing forests. 90% have been destroyed already.

"The other aspect is the socio-economic impact. One major mining company has a black mark over its activities in Madagascar because of burgeoning syphilis around where it is active.

"Madagascar has a very low rate of HIV infection, so if you bring in foreigners there are added risks and we have to very careful about that. You could easily expose the local population to new diseases."

Use your own creativity
Sir Tom Farmer, Kwik-Fit

Kwik-Fit was one of the most cherished UK brands of the 1980s, yet founder Sir Tom Farmer never wasted money on expensive advertising agencies. Everything from the name to the irritatingly catchy TV jingle were conceived by either Farmer himself or one of his senior managers.

"I thought about the fad to spell words wrongly, like 'KOOKERS' and 'KLEENED', so I spelt 'quick fit', Kwik-Fit. You would have to pay somebody millions of pounds to create that name.

"We started Kwik-Fit in 1971 and it grew from one place in Edinburgh, yet within three years I was approached by an organisation that wanted to buy us out. One of the things that really propelled us was the advertising program for the 'Kwik-Fit fitter'. Our advertising man sat scribbling for an hour then announced, 'I've got something'; he wrote on the board 'You can't get better than a Kwik-Fit fitter'.

"Then we came up with the musical TV ads, which we knew would be a winner with television, but we didn't predict the impact on our staff, either. All of a sudden they went from being a fitter to being a Kwik-Fit fitter."

Become a sought-after brand
Max Clifford, PR

It goes without saying that personal branding is critical to the sustainability of Max Clifford Associates. He is a TV regular and can express an opinion on most subjects.

Clifford believes that building a personal brand, even at a local level, will help you grow your business. You should take all media opportunities that come along and try to generate some of your own.

"My personal brand is very important to my business. Today I have done 15 different interviews on different subjects, and it averages about 30 or 40 a week.

"That's wonderful as long as you don't make a complete fool of yourself. The more you do it the more you are invited back because they don't have to spend 30 seconds establishing who you are.

"Charlie Mullins is one of my clients and does very well from celebrities. We created the Buster brand from one of his employees and Pimlico's got hundreds of thousands of pounds worth of business from that.

"It's a very good example of the benefits of being able to tap into the popular media."

Online PR's golden rule: be honest

Steve Leach, Bigmouthmedia

Online marketing and PR is partly about increasing your brand awareness and partly to do with managing your company's reputation, says Bigmouthmedia's Steve Leach. Blogs and forums are unregulated so you have to make sure your brand is talked about in a positive way.

That's not easy, however, especially because online opinion-formers do not always behave rationally. The important thing is to engage with people and be honest about who you are – don't pretend to be a neutral web user if you're actually defending your company.

"It's better to address these things head-on. It is a very, very diverse and unregulated environment so you're not dealing with entircly rational people all the time. Sometimes you can be very rational, play by all the rules and deliver exactly what people want and they will just tear you up – it can be very damaging for a brand. The more positive flip-side is about influence.

"We never do any of the covert stuff on blogs or forums, we actually represent the brand either as Bigmouth or as the client itself. Most people online are looking for recognition themselves so why not give feedback and let the bloggers know that it has been a very positive experience."

Think twice about PR for PR's sake

Syed Ahmed, *The Apprentice*

Syed Ahmed didn't go on *The Apprentice* for the fame, but he suffered the full media backlash when he was fired from the show. Soon after, he was forced to dodge the cameras when it was revealed he had started a relationship with fellow contestant Michelle Dewberry.

"PR can be damaging. If your strategy is to go out there and get as much PR as possible then you're in for a surprise because you often have no control over it. Journalists sometimes like me and sometimes don't.

"It's part and parcel of going on a TV show. It was difficult after the show because I lost all privacy and people say what they like. I was a journalist's dream coming off the back of *The Apprentice*, and having a relationship with Michelle. It was a very sensitive and difficult time.

"But you grow up very quickly and you become a much stronger person; it prepares you very well for life."

PR can make you credible
Rob Shreeve, One Alfred Place

Rob Shreeve worked as managing director at Virgin for ten years, so he picked up a thing or two from Sir Richard Branson's approach to PR. The greatest self-publicist of them all established an airline against all the odds because of his swashbuckling endeavours.

Risking his life with daredevil escapades brought Branson massive television exposure and incalculable marketing value. Today he's drawing similar press attention by making Virgin Galactic a front-runner in the tourism space race.

"Virgin Atlantic was an instinctive feeling of how an airline should be, how it could be different, how the staff could be different, how you could promote yourself and Richard had the huge benefit of being a great publicist with a ready-made audience.

"When the airline started, there was this great reaction of how could somebody who makes records run an airline? There was a big credibility issue, so what does Richard do? He starts crossing the Atlantic in various ways; he has a powerboat crossing breaking records, he does a balloon crossing and it's all building up that credibility with huge PR.

"Everyone's watching the Virgin Atlantic balloon on the news, so it gets millions and millions of pounds worth of publicity. Now it's a Virgin icon and it's become associated with all the right kind of emotions and ideas."

MISTAKES AND FAILURE

Growth isn't forever

Ashley Ward, NEXEC Partners, Wharfedale, Orchestream

Ashley Ward's first business was liquidated despite starting out life as a successful, growing enterprise. The company, which sold computer software, flourished in the early 1980s but sloppy licensing deals, unsustainable growth and (he admits) his own arrogance resulted in the business closing down.

Ward's error was to convince himself that once a company was growing it could continue indefinitely, and once that was achieved the business was safe. He ignored warning signals, including the fact that he was the only senior manager, and it cost him the business.

"I built the business up, floated it and broke it. I made every mistake possible...not least failing to realise that growth isn't linear, it's variable. I grew too big, too quick, too flat – there was me and 70 people below me, so no hierarchy to speak of, and I surrounded myself with advisors who were basically leaches.

"One thing I did right was quit while I was ahead. After a licensing deal went wrong with one of our core products I realised the writing was on the wall, and although it had at one time in the past been making a lot of money we knew it was time to stop."

Don't believe your own hype

Brad Burton, 4Networking

Brad Burton's biggest mistake with 4Networking was what he refers to as his "Walt Disney moment". Having established dozens of breakfast meeting events in one area of England, he decided to stop actively recruiting new attendees, believing that word of mouth would be enough.

"We had a big area managers' meeting and I said, 'We're not going to ask people to join any more, we're just going to give them a form and that's it!' I was spending hard on merchandising, everyone had adopted this model and nobody was applying to join. I had overspent, so it was close to falling over just based on my whim.

"It was like a Rubik's cube with two sides messed up; I shook it and then all the sides were wrong, instead of just sorting out the two that were bad. Then I had to work out how to get it back to normal. We had to juggle our finances, and juggle the invoices. Now I'm much more cautious."

Consultants are not always right
Dame Mary Perkins, Specsavers

Specsavers hasn't made too many mistakes in its journey from start-up to multinational brand, but founder Dame Mary Perkins admits one or two mishaps did take place. However, she claims the worst errors were those committed by consultants working for the firm, not the firm itself.

"There weren't any serious mistakes, but there was one clanger in the Netherlands. We used consultants, and they didn't report back correctly; there was already a low-priced business established which they missed and it caused us a lot of problems.

"They also said we couldn't use our British name because the Dutch wouldn't understand it. We used a different name for the first two stores and it was rubbish. We couldn't wait to change it to Specsavers. It was a waste of time and money, but we learned a valuable lesson about branding."

Don't let a mistake turn into a disaster
David Gold, Ann Summers

David Gold says his biggest mistake was holding on to a business that was costing him money. His advice to entrepreneurs is to be ruthless with businesses that are not working. Know when to quit and when you do, act decisively.

"I published a magazine called *Bite*, which was an Ann Summers-orientated product, and the first edition got good reviews, but because it was Ann Summers it struggled to get serious advertisers. But I persevered with it – and ended up with a million pound loss.

"We'd invested a million pounds; and the most painful thing was pulling the plug. It was a mistake; I ran it for too long, I should have cut my losses in the first year instead of going on for two years. But you become attached to your product and your belief that you're right becomes quite strong."

Gold says it's vitally important that you exit a business with some of your capital intact. The worst thing an inexperienced entrepreneur can do is throw good money after bad until all financial options are exhausted.

"To fail and try again is important, so you never want to lose everything. It's a bit like the gambler who goes into the nightclub and he puts £100 in his back pocket. He's got £200 in total, but that £100 is his cab fare and his ability to pay his hotel bill. The fool is the one who takes that £100 out as well and gambles it. People often say, 'That's the entrepreneur', but I think 'That's the mug, the failed entrepreneur.'"

Be prepared to admit defeat
Brad Burton, 4Networking

Brad Burton founded a marketing firm that was struggling to develop a client base. When it became obvious he was not making enough to live on, the 4Networking entrepreneur took a job as a pizza-delivery boy. Far from regretting that decision, he now feels it was the best course of action he could have taken.

"It was a cathartic experience. I thought, 'Now that I have hit rock bottom, how do I get out of this?' I've got a brain, drive and ambition, so why am I failing? How many people are like me? Or am I the world's unluckiest man?'

"And bang! I came up with the idea for a networking group. I created the website that day. I used to be so embarrassed about that episode, but now I see it as a badge of honour."

Don't mix business with pleasure
Deborah Meaden, *Dragons' Den*

Deborah Meaden's first business was exporting glass and ceramics from Italy to the UK. She acted as an agency, connecting the Italian manufacturers and the British retailers. The business failed because, although Meaden signed contracts protecting herself, the manufacturers and retailers quickly cut her out of the chain.

Meaden says it was the right decision to abort the business before it bankrupted her, but she admits that her original motivation for starting up was misguided; she allowed her love of Italy to influence her decision.

"My motivation for starting that business was partly that it was such a lovely business to run. I had friends in Italy and my thought was, 'What business could I set up so that I could have links with Italy and travel there?' So I guess you could say I started it for the wrong reasons.

"My biggest mistake was failing to realise how quickly the companies could cut me out as a middleman. It is not okay to fail; it can be a good experience but you shouldn't think 'So what? I tried'. It should hurt. Then you should learn from it, pick yourself up and say 'I'm not going to make that mistake again'."

A failure is sometimes salvageable

Doug Richard, *Dragons' Den*

Doug Richard has experienced his fair share of entrepreneurial failure as well as startling successes. His research business, Library House, was liquidated and several of his investments have not delivered the kind of growth or financial return he hoped for.

But Richard knows when to quit and when to carry on. When his mobile social media business, Trutap, was struggling, he scaled back staff numbers dramatically, cut costs and took a fresh look at the business plan. Having turned the business around he's now looking to re-recruit many of the previous team members.

"Its timing wasn't particularly great because it preceded the iPhone by just enough to miss that particular boat. But having said that it became fairly successful in its own right and we're in the process of restoring the team and growing it again. It's not my best start-up, I admit, but it's certainly not my worst.

"With tech start-ups especially, sometimes the world turns in a different direction than we all forecast. That happens all the time. You think, 'We're going to go there and that's where the future is' and it turns out that it's not.

"That's the biggest challenge in the early days. Sometimes the tech doesn't work, sometimes the founders have their heads screwed on wrong, sometimes we just make bad decisions. Early-stage tech companies fail for a lot of reasons; sometimes it's the wrong time in the cycle, sometimes somebody else did a better job. It's a shame, but it happens."

Mistakes are a reality of business

James Caan, *Dragons' Den*, Hamilton Bradshaw

For James Caan, mistakes are unavoidable in business. Despite his estimated £70m fortune, the *Dragons' Den* entrepreneur has never developed a business without encountering ups and downs. For him, talented entrepreneurs do not avoid problems, they just deal with issues better than others.

"It wasn't plain sailing for me. I have never been fortunate enough to run a business that has delivered without any problems. I'm a strong believer that in business anything that can go wrong generally will go wrong.

"You should succeed if you can anticipate all the issues that you will face. Not just sales or financial, but governance, cultural challenges, operating in different markets, functions, relationships, currency, taxation – they are all things that you will face when developing a business."

Your people will get you back on your feet
Mark Constantine, Lush

When Mark Constantine's Cosmetics to Go business went bust he was ready to throw in the towel as an entrepreneur. He still had close ties to his staff, suppliers, bank and potential investors, but despite all that it took encouragement from his old team to convince the Lush founder to try again.

"There's a statistic about people going bust; about 60% either have a heart attack or a breakdown so it must be a fairly big strain. I didn't seem to have either of those problems but it wasn't a great time.

"I wouldn't have started again if it hadn't been for my colleagues; I really didn't feel like picking myself up at all. It doesn't matter who you are, you're only as good as the people you work with; the whole culture of suggesting that entrepreneurs are able to somehow create these big things on their own is total bullshit.

"You don't lose everything when you fail in business because you have the people you work with, you have the product ideas and you have a relationship with the suppliers. Even though I lost £2m, they wanted to do business with me again. Their rationale was, 'We've done business with you for 17 years and the fact that you lost money doesn't mean we wouldn't work with you again'.

"The banks were keen to help and provide a line of credit again and customers were knocking on the door of the empty building and shouting through the letterbox. It was quite bizarre, especially when you're feeling totally awful. When we did start again we got this tremendous wave of support and I was incredibly grateful."

Don't get carried away by a booming market
Mark Zaleski, DailyMotion

Mark Zaleski experienced failure with US dotcom giant Webvan. Like other website implosions of the boom years, Webvan spent vast amounts of money on its equipment, staff and operations but couldn't match the big bucks going out with the sales coming in.

Zaleski says the lesson from the dotcom boom period is that every business, no matter how much it is hyped, has a real value based on sales and profits. On that basis Webvan was hugely overvalued by investors.

"We had the lavish HQ, it wasn't as bad as Boo.com – it wasn't mad in that sense – but there was a conviction that we would be worth $100bn and it was our God-given right. But it wasn't. We needed to prove the concept and not just spread the idea like crazy.

"We were told, 'We'll get you the cash, don't worry about it – it's important to be first to market and build up your footprint'. That didn't seem right to me as you can't get something for nothing, people want a return on their cash.

"We had money in the bank and we could give it back if it didn't work out, but the VCs thought we had enough cash to work through the problems – that's where it was flawed but that was the general sentiment at the time."

If all else fails, cut your loses
Rupert Clevely, Geronimo Inns

It hasn't always been a smooth ride for Rupert Clevely's Geronimo Inns. While the business has grown at a steady rate overall, an early cash-flow blip accentuated by an accidental brush with the mafia nearly ended the business. Clevely's advice is to cut your loses when the odds stack up against you.

"At the time of our first investment we had had some trouble and the money was as much to shore up as to expand. We had a pub in the East End which was awful, there were problems with the local mafia and we had ghastly times hiding behind the bar and guys standing at the door with guns in their pockets.

"That wasn't a good time at all and we had to write off some of the debt. I think one of the biggest mistakes that people make is not to cut their losses."

Mistakes are common in property development
Sarah Beeny, *Property Ladder*, Tepilo.com

Sarah Beeny is famous for being a celebrity property developer, although this is just one part of her business portfolio. Nevertheless, her experience in the home improvement industry has taught her many lessons, and she has lots of insights for people hoping to make money from property.

"It's a lot better entering when the property market is subdued rather than at the top. The developers that enter at the top and ride it down get badly burned. But as I've always said, get your figures absolutely right. Don't be optimistic about how much you're going to sell it for or how much it is going to cost or how long it's going to take.

"That's the biggest mistake people make – they almost take their perceived sale value and work back from there. They say it'll cost

£2,000 to re-roof and rewire a six-bedroom house because that's what they want it to cost, and then they have to sell it for £300,000 more than any other house in the area because they want to make some money. It's simply not going to happen!

"You have to be careful not to make a house bland and boring, but if it's a business then it's a business and if it's a home it's a home. People get muddled between the two. If you're designing a house for other people then do it for other people."

Don't be fooled by flashy things that don't work
Ashley Ward, NEXEC Partners, Wharfedale, Orchestream

Ashley Ward says the latest round of internet businesses will struggle to make money and that entrepreneurs should think carefully about setting up an online business that doesn't fulfil an obvious need. Equally, entrepreneurs who have exited their businesses should think twice before investing in new technology.

"A lot of businesses starting up today are hit or miss. People of my generation find it almost impossible to tell what is going to be a winner, because we don't know how the modern teenager thinks.

"Most businesses are variants on a theme. Plenty of social networking sites have started up, but they all demand a huge volume of users and there's only so much the market can take. The price per user is buttons – so to get it right is incredibly hard.

"The attrition rate for new start-ups is going to be higher than we've ever seen before. A lot of people investing in those will take a bath because people don't actually need most of them and in the end people use what they need."

MONEY

Keep profits in the business

Adrian Moorhouse, Lane4

Adrian Moorhouse's Lane4 never took on investment and channelled profits back into the business to fund growth. Moorhouse sees money as a gauge of success, but doesn't draw cash out of the business to fund an expensive lifestyle.

He says the only time he plans to refinance the business is when he eventually sells it, preferably in a management buyout to his senior team. He believes succession is important in so much as you must be careful who the business goes to and whether they care about its objectives.

"I didn't want it to be a lifestyle business, so from the word go the model encompassed longevity and legacy. A lot of owner-managers retain control, won't let go and take profits for themselves. We didn't take a dividend for 10 years and rolled all the profits back into the business. A lot of people who start businesses put their expenses through it. That's not for me.

"If profit goes out every year then there may not be enough investment to drive the business forward. So we reinvested in the early days to make sure it wasn't a flash in the pan – it's very important to keep cash in the business. If you want to do something growth-wise, why get investment when you can invest in it yourself using your own profits?"

Don't be afraid to sell if it's the right thing to do
Craig Sams, Green & Black's

In 1999, Craig Sams sold a whopping 75% of Green & Black's to the founders of the New Covent Garden Soup Company. The decision was fuelled by a need to market the already popular product and Sams was unable to self-fund a large promotional campaign.

The problem was much of the business' cash reserves were tied up in stock and no amount of invoice discounting could free up enough cash to spend on marketing. (Invoice discounting is an arrangement where (usually) your bank 'buys' invoices from you and, for a fee, chases up your debts. It means you get paid quickly and don't have to worry about late or default payments.) Despite relinquishing such a large stake in his business, the investors' money in turn made his share extremely valuable.

"They took 75% of the business and injected a lot of capital so that we could really invest. We all knew that if you spent money on marketing it paid itself back many times over, but you have to get the money from somewhere and the bank was financing us to the absolute maximum through invoice discounting.

"The main consideration was that the 25% of the business we sold to Cadbury in 2005 was worth many times the value of the business we had at the beginning of 1999 when we sought the investment. So that was the simple trade-off, and it was very much worth it."

Don't be wasteful with your cash
Brad Burton, 4Networking

Brad Burton takes a philosophical approach towards money. Of course it's a nice thing to have, but he flatly refuses to give away equity in 4Networking just so he can spoil himself with executive perks. He'd much prefer to allocate equity to loyal staff as a motivational tool.

"Someone offered to invest £300,000 once, but I thought apart from having a Range Rover Sport with 4N livery on the side what am I going to do with it? My motivation isn't money, it's making a difference.

"When I had no money I used to think my goal was earning money because I needed it. Don't get me wrong I like expensive toys and holidays, but not at the expense of making a difference. Some people in business lack that motivation."

Pick investors you can be friendly with

Deborah Meaden, *Dragons' Den*

Deborah Meaden says she had an overwhelmingly positive relationship with Phoenix Equity Partners, who invested in her business Weststar Holiday Parks. From her experience with the firm she learned the importance of good relations between the business' management team and their backers.

Meaden applied lessons learned from this experience to her own investing strategy on TV show *Dragons' Den*. She firmly believes entrepreneurs should find investors who they get on with, not just those with the deepest pockets.

"It is absolutely essential to be a fair investor as well as a shrewd one. I don't want to work with people who are not happy with the deal. I really appreciated my time with Phoenix, I found them extremely good to work alongside; they were honest and if things had to change we discussed it and we made the decision together.

"I never once felt 'I wish I hadn't done this'. Through their behaviour I learned the things that made me happy and I'm very keen that other people think the same way when I invest in them. I think about the deal and I offer what I think is fair, because there are two parties involved."

Crunch those numbers
Gil Steyaert, Adidas

Gil Steyaert is a great believer in facts and figures. There are many ways to measure a business' progress and growth but financial data doesn't lie, especially when numbers are collected together in a methodical way and used to calculate targets and performance over time.

"If you give me five years of profit-and-loss and balance sheets, I can probably tell you more about your business than you can tell me. Numbers talk and that's how you measure your success. You can qualify results, you can explain them, but in the end numbers are truthful.

"I read a lot in business and I do value key performance indicators. They tell me how much I need to spend and what I gain. It is all about keeping your eyes on measurement and performance, and where you're going. Try to put everything you do into numbers."

Prepare before you pitch
James Caan, *Dragons' Den*, Hamilton Bradshaw

Pitching for investment is a skill very close to James Caan's heart. He has seen hundreds of pitches through *Dragons' Den* and via his own private-equity firm, Hamilton Bradshaw, and feels the best pitches are by people who understand their market, get the figures right and have a clear set of goals.

The really bad pitches are by people who fail to plan, don't have a strong entrepreneurial background and who cannot explain why their product will sell. Caan is less worried about the product itself; he thinks an average product executed well is more valuable than a great product executed poorly.

"What makes a good pitch? It's the passion of the individual. I think the individual has to be in the right stage of life and have the right level of experience. They need to have the right motivations too. For me, business is all about the entrepreneur themselves.

"The worst pitches are when individuals have done a poor amount of research, they have come up with a valuation which has no rhyme or reason and they have no concept of how they will sell their product(s) to the market because they don't know what their market is."

Be careful with your cash flow
Craig Sams, Green & Black's

Throughout his business career Craig Sams has manipulated his cash flow and stock to improve his financial standing. In the 1980s with Whole Earth Foods he reduced the company turnover from millions to hundreds of thousands in order to sell off stock and clear his debts.

As the business grew he used invoice discounting to preserve cash flow and keep the business healthy.

"The main problem that I've had to overcome was cash flow. You have to stay on top of that. When the business expanded, invoice discounting made growth much easier and it kept us going until well into the late 1990s, helping us to handle our increasing stock-holding costs.

"I worked out that if we reduced the amount of stock we were holding, we could pay off our debts and have a nice profitable business. We had a £3.5m turnover and I dropped it to £800,000. The company went straight into profit and we had loads of cash from liquidating our stock so I could pay off bank debt and our investors."

Start on a shoestring
Jennifer Irvine, The Pure Package

When Jennifer Irvine founded The Pure Package, she did so on a shoestring. The food-delivery business had two main overheads in the beginning: ingredients and transportation. The other tools required to start a business – the sink, fridge and oven – were already in Irvine's kitchen.

Starting a business can be a costly process if you need to hire staff, rent office space and buy equipment. Some of Britain's best businesses began on a budget of close to zero and grew from sheer man (or woman) power.

"I don't like stress; I try to avoid it   I think it's overrated, so I set my business up from the kitchen sink, quite literally.

"If you start a business and you have to set up a really expensive kitchen (or whatever is required), install new computer systems and employ lots of people, etc, then most people need to get a bank loan or get outside investors involved, but that's not what I did."

If you don't need it, don't spend it
Kanya King, MOBO Awards

Like many entrepreneurs, Kanya King was able to establish and grow her business by keeping costs at bargain basement levels. By cutting out non-essential costs, including a proper office and paid employees, King was able to create the first MOBO event on budget and on time.

"Nobody needed to know that we didn't have fancy offices. That made sense to me because I wanted to keep our overheads very low. It meant for a time that we conducted meetings in coffee shops but it was essential in the early days."

Reinvest your profits wisely
Kavita Oberoi, Oberoi Consulting

Once they start making money, most entrepreneurs re-invest in their business in order to make it grow. Kavita Oberoi is no different, but because her cost base is low she has scope to invest in interests unrelated to her core business. This, she says, gives her a chance to make additional revenue without overexerting herself.

"I'm setting up other businesses along the way. I think it's a good direction for my company to go in. It's one thing making money but how many people can make that money grow? From the start I've been very keen, where the profitability's there, to reinvest.

"People say it's not a good time to buy but I've just bought commercial property which already has tenants in for the next five years. There are opportunities and interest rates are low, so we're aware and looking for new business."

Pitch for the full amount, not a penny more or less
Sam Malin, Madagascar Oil

Having secured huge amounts of funding for his businesses, Sam Malin has identified a rule for securing investment. According to him it is better to pitch for a full total in one go, than to return to investors cap in hand for new amounts.

"I have noticed that it takes the same amount of time to raise £500,000 as it does to raise – and this is a real example – £100m. You have to prove a worthy allocation of funds; it's no good asking for £100m when it's clear £5m is enough.

"As long as you get funding that matches the project it seems to take about the same amount of time. Making sure that you raise sufficient funding for a particular project is important, it doesn't save time to say I'll raise a smaller number now and then try again next year."

Save two months' worth of salaries
Keith Potts, Jobsite

In the early days Keith Potts worried about his business' financial position and it wasn't until he took on investment that he relaxed and felt comfortable enough to spend. But he doesn't regret those hard-up days; on the contrary, he feels it was a great experience.

"The main problem is trying not to run out of cash. Our chairman, who'd been in business many years, told us to retain a two-month salary buffer. If we didn't make a single penny for two months, we'd still be able to pay the salaries. So we saved two months' pay. But that impacts on the business; I want to spend that money! We might need to do a viral marketing campaign, go on the radio or produce some posters.

"So when our investors came in, part of that deal was not just ring-fencing the cash for the shareholders, it was to put a £5m lump sum into a bank account that we didn't have to ask permission to spend. We used a fraction of it yet it gave us was the confidence to spend like mad on the kind of marketing we needed to do.

"Now I feel that the best situation that you could ever possibly be in when starting out is not having any money. If you don't have money then you become very creative."

Research different ways to fund your business
Lord Bilimoria, Cobra Beer

When Lord Bilimoria founded Cobra Beer he employed a range of strategies to fund the business without giving away any of his equity. A trained accountant, he was well placed to pick and choose from the various financial instruments available, from government grants to invoice finance.

Most entrepreneurs aren't so fortunate to have an encyclopaedic knowledge of funding packages, but the principle of retaining ownership of your business is still valid. Bilimoria recommends thoroughly researching all your options before picking one particular route.

"Raising money was always a challenge: getting the first overdrafts and the government's small-firms loans was very important. It was always a challenge to hold on to equity and not give away stakes in the business. I got around that by raising money through a whole range of resources from bills of exchange to letters of credit."

Even if you have cash, spend it wisely
Martha Lane Fox, Lastminute.com

Unlike the vast majority of dotcom-boom businesses, Latminute.com was extremely careful with its cash. While bosses at other websites lavished their firms with unnecessary perks, co-founder Martha Lane Fox continued to do basic admin chores in order to save money.

"I remember my dad coming to meet me and I was still in the office on a Sunday night at 11.30pm. I was writing cheques for each individual person for their salary and writing something about a good thing they had done that month.

"He asked, 'Do you really think you should be doing that?' and I said, 'Yes'. He said, 'Why don't you hire someone else to do that, it might be a better use of your time!' That idea seemed impossible to me."

Get paid upfront
Max Clifford, PR

Most entrepreneurs would argue that a contract is the safest way to guarantee getting paid. Max Clifford works differently. He bypasses the payment problem by asking for cash upfront.

"Get paid in advance; I was always have. It makes sense because if you're not paid you don't start working; that's worked very well for me over the last 40 years. It's good for cash flow and it helps to keep admin to a minimum."

Investment works for fast-growing businesses
Rupert Clevely, Geronimo Inns

The most important reason to take on investment, says Rupert Clevely, is to facilitate quick growth in your business that could not be achieved without an influx of cash. His business was growing steadily with a few new pubs every year, but after post-investment the growth rate accelerated quickly.

"This business couldn't go on growing through new freehold sites, because every time I open a new pub, it costs a lot of money. If I open a restaurant in the King's Road and buy the bricks and mortar it'll cost between £1.5m and £3m. Where am I going to find that money?

"If I get it from trading it might only be one year's trading I have available in terms of free cash by the time I've paid the bank, etc., so how can I expand and grow my business? I can't do that very quickly. So either I've got to bring money into the company or I sell and leave it to somebody else to grow the business, which I've no plans to do yet."

Understand who invests in what
Sam Malin, Madagascar Oil

Securing funding for major projects is what Sam Malin does best. As founder of Madagascar Oil he won hundreds of millions of pounds worth of investment. Dealing with such high stakes it is critical for him to find the right investors and to deliver the perfect pitch.

For Malin banks are a no-no. His brand of high-risk venture is far beyond what most financial institutions would consider putting their money behind. His advice to entrepreneurs is to find the right form of investment for your business.

"A high-street bank does not want to countenance the sort of risk profile they are presented with and the bureaucracy is enormous – they want a level of data that would be difficult to put together for an early stage project.

"The kind of funders we go to want presentations and financial data but there are still a few out there who will act solely on gut feeling; you never get that from a high-street bank."

You really can start up on a shoestring
Wayne Hemingway, Red or Dead

Most new businesses that start up are small, and Red or Dead was no exception. Co-founder Wayne Hemingway launched it with little more than a few coins in his pocket. Times have moved on since then, but he remains convinced that being an entrepreneur needn't be a rich man's game.

"It's possible to start up in business with no money, if you have got an idea and you hit the zeitgeist of the time, which we did. We sold second-hand clothes on Camden market at a time when people were starting to wear that sort of thing.

"At the time these clothes were still a thing you searched for in jumble sales, so a couple of us went round jumble sales buying everything we could that looked cool and stuck it on a market stall. We didn't need any money, just a few 10ps in our pocket. That's all it used to cost."

PEOPLE AND EMPLOYEES

Your first recruits are critical
Ajaz Ahmed, AKQA

Your most critical recruits are the first two people you hire, according to AKQA's Ajaz Ahmed. If they have the right skills, the right level of commitment and their objectives are in line with those of the business, then you have a much greater chance of surviving.

Ahmed's first hire was a software developer, but he put a very specific remit to the headhunter to find the right candidate. He wanted someone with an engineer's mindset, not a developer's.

"It sounds obvious but I always tell entrepreneurs that the team you put together in the beginning is the most important element of success in your business. When we hired our first technology director we asked the headhunter to find us an engineer who understood software.

"With engineering, the tolerance of mistakes is closer to zero than it is with software. I don't subscribe to the idea that all software has bugs. I want great code, immaculate with close attention to detail in everything – when you launch a product you should want it to be perfect."

Identify what people are good at
Anthony Ganjou, Curb

Many of the people who work for Anthony Ganjou's creative agency, Curb, are independent artists and not full-time employees. The business' role is to introduce their skills to advertisers and to coordinate the contract between the artist and the client.

Not having a full-time staff saves Curb money and lends the business flexibility, but it means Ganjou must direct plenty of energy towards recruiting and managing the freelance artists, so that jobs are fulfilled to standards demanded by his clients.

"We're trying to pull all the different elements together to make a shortcut for agencies that want to do something professional and that works."

Find the business' knowledge bank
Ashley Ward, NEXEC Partners, Wharfedale, Orchestream

If you are buying into a business with existing staff, as Ashley Ward did, it's a good idea to find the person who is most knowledgeable about the business and learn all you can from them. Ward says you should use their knowledge to formulate your own plans.

"When I bought Wharfedale there was a marketing guy who had a really warped view of how to make it work: distribution, pricing, the lot. He was wrong but he knew his way around the industry like no one else. So I attached him to my hip and then applied my own rule, which was go out to the market, seeing dealers and asking what they thought of the company and how could we do it better."

Hire older people
Charlie Mullins, Pimlico Plumbers

Charlie Mullins of Pimlico Plumbers swears by hiring older (and more experienced) staff. Mullins opted to recruit Mario, who has more than 50 years' experience in working environments, as his PA. He has also employed the UK's oldest worker: 102-year-old Buster Martin.

"We have lots of older people working as valets and in admin roles, there's no substitute for experience and Mario has years of it. He's a great PA who can think for himself, unlike some younger people who are starting work for the first time.

"Experience makes for a better workplace and people look up to the older members of staff, picking up tips all the time, and I think old and young people make a great mixture. If you get that right then you've got a winning formula."

Hire the best, regardless of cost
Ashley Ward, NEXEC Partners, Wharfedale, Orchestream

According to Ashley Ward, the best businesses hire the best people, regardless of cost. He believes hiring on price – or saving money on the salaries of new recruits – is a false economy which will end up costing you more money than you save.

Having closed his first business, Ward himself was hired by a company that undervalued him. He took the job, but used it as a vehicle to pay the bills while looking out for his next entrepreneurial opportunity.

"No business I've ever been involved with has ever succeeded by hiring on price. Two guys: one asking for £60k, one for £70k. They hire the £60k guy even though often a 10% reduction in price means an 80% reduction in quality. Hire the best people possible, because they will make the business work."

Ask for time before money from investors
Doug Richard, *Dragons' Den*

As a celebrity investor, famous for his turn on the BBC's *Dragons' Den*, Doug Richard has put money behind numerous entrepreneurs. But he argues that the relationship between investor and entrepreneur is as important as the money itself.

For entrepreneurs looking for funding from a business angel, he suggests taking a 'pre-investment trial' to see whether you bond and whether you can reasonably expect to develop a mutually beneficial relationship. The alternative is jumping in with investment, which could lead to problems later on.

"It's my view that as an angel investor I should work with people before I invest to make sure that we can work together. If you're going to work with an angel investor, he or she should be willing to put in some time upfront for free.

"It can be incredibly valuable for the entrepreneur as well as the investor. Both parties' risk goes down enormously. The alternative is two strangers wondering whether it's going to work out and real money being involved before they get to know each other."

Develop your friends base
Gerry Calabrese, The Hoxton Pony

They say it's not what you know, but who you know and Hoxton Pony founder Gerry Calabrese is living proof. His rise through the ranks to become owner of one of East London's favourite nightspots has been accelerated by his abilities as a networker and friend-maker.

Calabrese is a serial entrepreneur who has also launched a high-end gin brand with friend Andy Pearson and bought into his doorman's security company. Calabrese has developed a loyal group of friends and it seems he wouldn't go into business without them.

"I think one of the most important elements in how I've got to this stage so quickly is the relationships that I've kindled along the way. A lot of people who are working with me now have been with me for eight years or so. My investors have come through contacts too. The son of one of them was a regular at a bar I used to run."

Older people are a mine of good advice
David Gold, Ann Summers

Older people offer a wealth of experience and retired entrepreneurs make some of the best mentors to fledgling entrepreneurs, according to David Gold. He says young people in business should recruit retirees as advisors, because they will benefit from an older person's knowledge.

"What is the strength of an older person? It's their experience. Is that important? Yes, it's massively important. A retired businessman is a most valuable asset because he can say, 'You don't have to do it that way; I can remember that happening to me, don't go down that route. Reconsider it'."

Focus on teams, not individuals
Gil Steyaert, Adidas

Adidas' Gil Steyaert believes it is teamwork that drives businesses forward. Great people don't necessarily work well together and a talented but fractured team is less productive than a cohesive and cooperative one full of average people.

"There is a cliché that people are the most valuable assets in business. It's correct but not perfect, for me it's teamwork. You can have great individuals but it's of little help if they refuse to work in teams. Your biggest advantage is if your people work together."

The more people you have, the simpler the message must be
Ian Powell, PricewaterhouseCoopers

PricewaterhouseCoopers chief Ian Powell says one of his biggest challenges is setting out a vision for the business and communicating it to his 16,000 staff in the UK. But he has learned that as the number of people you manage grows, the simpler the message has to be.

"The biggest challenge is getting the emotional impact into the overall vision for the business. Everyone has objectives set every year and we have to ensure that these are in line with the overall goal. It means masses of communication.

"The capacity for misinterpretation is pretty immense. If you convey something at the top of an organisation by the time it gets to everyone it can be badly out of synch – it's like building a skyscraper in reverse: if you get it an inch out at the bottom it will be 10 metres wrong at the top."

"It's good, direct communication in language people understand. Every morning there's a little box that appears at the bottom of employees' screens containing PwC news. We introduced it a year ago and the hit rate is 85%, average stay time is about three minutes. Keep it relevant, short, punchy and of interest."

Hire people who are better than you
Martha Lane Fox, Lastminute.com

Like most entrepreneurs with a history of great businesses, Martha Lane Fox values people power enormously. She believes in hiring the best people, even if their skill sets outshine her own.

"Hire phenomenal people. I always try and hire people that are better than me. Don't feel threatened by that, instead create a culture that has fabulous people in it."

Surround yourself with people who'll ground you
Rupert Clevely, Geronimo Inns

Real entrepreneurs are by nature ambitious risk-takers who always want to make the most of the opportunities in front of them according to

Rupert Clevely. This is a personality trait of many great business builders.

But Clevely warns that entrepreneurs such as these must surround themselves with level-headed colleagues and support staff who act as the voice of reason when entrepreneurs get ahead of themselves and threaten to overstretch the business.

"An entrepreneur doesn't want to run a tiny business that's never going to grow, they want to try new ideas, develop the firm and take it from one place to another. In many cases they want to do it as quickly as possible.

"What I've tried to do in my business is surround myself with people to help put the reins on me and to steer me in the right direction, because otherwise I'd be like a runaway horse, doing a million things that would probably end up in a cloud of smoke."

Trust your staff, but evaluate them too
Kavita Oberoi, Oberoi Consulting

The majority of Kavita Oberoi's mistakes in business have been to do with hiring, training and firing staff. In the past she has experienced painful disloyalty from senior staff and freelance workers alike, and has recently implemented a formal appraisal system to prevent it happening again.

Oberoi says entrepreneurs should think hard before hiring freelancers, having experienced a hard time encouraging them to meet targets and generally motivating them as to the business' goals. She admits that on rare occasions both contractors and permanent staff stole ideas from the business and used them to set up rival firms.

Enthusiasm breeds enthusiasm
Dawn Gibbins, Flowcrete

According to Dawn Gibbins, people respond to an optimist. Her approach to people management is to inspire them with her gusto and enthusiasm for business. It works. She is one of Britain's most sought-after mentors and her new business, Barefoot Floors, is an altar of Zen-like calm.

"Enthusiasm is infectious. I've been doing a media circuit for press coverage and from that I've had quite a few people wanting me to mentor them. Since I set up Barefoot there are loads of people wanting to know where I get my energy from.

"They say, 'You're so inspirational', and when I ask them why, they say it's my positive attitude. I've been teaching that; you've got to be positive and you've got to find the things that give people a buzz."

Throw out the CVs
Wayne Hemingway, Red or Dead

Red or Dead's co-founder Wayne Hemingway doesn't believe in business plans, so it's no surprise he doesn't believe in CVs either. He claims never to have read one. His businesses always hire on gut instinct and Hemingway argues that most people know who they will hire (or do business with) within a few minutes of meeting them.

"Red or Dead was a team of people who share our philosophy, and they came from various backgrounds. The guy who ran the day-to-day stuff was a college dropout who got kicked out for doing something wrong and that was never a problem for us. I've never looked at anyone's CV; you judge people straight away and think 'Are they right for us?'.

"Personality is very important, it's very rare to meet a successful person who has no personality and is an idiot. There aren't many, although the odd one slips through. If you're a dullard, you're not going to make it; well, you won't have major success anyway.

"I do talks at business conferences and people ask me questions, and I know straightaway, although I don't say it, that they've no chance. Sorry. It's a combination of their products and themselves."

PLANNING AND STRATEGY

Concentrate on what works
Craig Sams, Green & Black's

Before husband and wife team Craig Sams and Josephine Fairley launched the ubiquitous chocolate brand Green & Black's, Sams ran a series of different businesses. Having dipped his toe into retail, wholesale and imports he eventually simplified his portfolio and focused on Whole Earth Foods, which had the greatest potential.

Sams' decision to focus his business interests allowed him to concentrate on the things that worked and the products that gave him the best return. The decision to close a business is a tough one, he says, but necessary if it serves the greater good.

"When Whole Earth Foods was taking off, we sold our restaurant to one of our customers. It was the same with the retail outlet. In 1982 we split the business three ways and I carried on producing just jam and peanut butter. Gradually a whole range emerged.

"Whole Earth Foods was so all-consuming; it had the greatest up-size potential. With that type of business you can reach everybody in the world or at least everybody in the country, whereas a shop is generally limited to its catchment area, and a restaurant even more so."

Revisit your strategy and be prepared to adapt
Anthony Ganjou, Curb

Anthony Ganjou's Curb is still a young business but, as one of the first entrants into its market, is growing rapidly. Fast growth means Ganjou must plan ahead sooner than most entrepreneurs would expect to, especially in areas such as international growth, which he wants to achieve as soon as possible.

For this reason he says his strategy is all-important; in particular he wants to see problems before they arise and avoid surprises in the future. He revisits his plans regularly, and recalculates his path allowing for the speed at which his business' landscape is changing.

"The next challenges are international growth while maintaining outstanding levels of customer service and delivery. We also have to stay one step ahead of the competition and define credibility in the media platforms that we create. I think those are the core challenges we face as a business.

"The nature of our growth so far means those challenges have come a lot sooner than we may have expected, but we've already put steps in place to make sure that we're on top of every single one of those challenges.

"I think that, especially at the moment, you've got to be pre-emptive in facing challenges. If you've got a business that's making an impact and is growing fast, you've got to expect that your competitors are going to try to do things better than you and you've always got to stay one step ahead."

If all else fails, try common sense
Charlie Mullins, Pimlico Plumbers

Charlie Mullins feels his strategy is rooted in common sense. The problem with common sense, he says, is that it's not very common. That's why, in his view, he was able to rise above other London-based plumbing companies during the 1980s.

The strategy is indeed simple: work out what people expect from a plumber and deliver it. Therefore, Pimlico strives to be prompt, professional, timely and transparent; attributes that are a must for most businesses but somehow passed the plumbing industry by for many years.

"I felt the industry had a bad reputation at the time: plumbers were always late, scruffy, making excuses, in dirty vans, and overcharging. I decided to do the opposite. There were so many obvious things and I don't know why other people hadn't tried to change the industry.

"If you're polite, respectful and do a good job then why would they go somewhere else? 80% of our customers have used us before. Some people say I discovered a gap in the market, but it was obvious to me. It's the same anywhere: if someone's late I'll be annoyed; if they're impolite I don't want them in my house; and if they're lying I don't want to do business with them. It stands to reason."

Prepare for retirement well in advance
David Gold, Ann Summers

Now in his seventies, Anne Summers' chief David Gold has one eye on the future of his business empire. He has no plans to retire just yet, but is only too aware of the odds against a business' survival if the founder fails to prepare for his succession.

"The more it fragments, the greater the risk to the business. In other words, if one person succeeds, there's a high success rate. If ten take over the business, I promise you it can't survive unless there's an understanding, or a dominant shareholder in the group. But if it's fragmented and everyone's got equal shares, the statistics tell me this isn't going to work.

"There was a big desire in my mind and in my heart to settle this for the sake of my family and for my own sake as well, because when I'm eventually out there at 95 watching the fish I want my business left in good hands."

Sell when the market's right, not when you are
Deborah Meaden, *Dragons' Den*

Soon after she bought Weststar Holiday Parks in a management buyout, Deborah Meaden was approached by a handful of investors who wanted to buy a stake in the business. While she hadn't planned on a quick sale, Meaden conceded that the market was ripe and prices were high.

"I received a lot of approaches but I had not acquired the business with the intention of selling it so quickly. However, this is advice I would give to people wondering whether to sell or not: the market doesn't always fit your timescale. It was clearly hotting up and there were a lot of people wanting in.

"Prices were going northward. If I had waited for my timing to be right I could have been selling when the market was in trouble."

Research the market thoroughly before expanding
Dame Mary Perkins, Specsavers

Specsavers is a global business with shops all over the world. Its co-founder, Dame Mary Perkins, has come up against several barriers in her efforts to spread the business outside the UK and has learned a considerable amount about the different expectations of customers in different countries.

Decisions ranging from the design of the shop displays to whether or not the firm should use its famous slogan, 'You should have gone to Specsavers', rest on national cultural proclivities. These, along with the various codes, rules and customs, have to be researched thoroughly before the business can set up in a new country.

"You've got to adapt to different cultures, and the product has to be different in subtle ways. The way people buy eye-care and eyewear varies quite a lot. But every country can learn a little from another country.

"Each of our countries has its own marketing director and some have completely different adverts, although they can share common elements such as photography. The slogan is global, where people speak English, but it doesn't always work as well as here – 'spek' means bacon in Dutch."

Stay nimble even if you grow big
Ian Powell, PricewaterhouseCoopers

Even a behemoth business like PricewaterhouseCoopers can move quickly and its chairman, Ian Powell, prides himself on the firm's manoeuvrability, which is rare in its industry. For Powell, being nimble is a great strength whatever the size of your business.

"We take qualities from smaller businesses. If you look at organisations of our size, if you're a market leader and you're not agile then you're just a target. If you're the market leader and you're agile then you have the strength of size but the nimbleness to adapt and evolve.

"You want all the benefits of massive scale and reach but you want to be able to move really quickly as well."

Know when planning has to stop
Gil Steyaert, Adidas

According to Gil Steyaert, making decisions is part and parcel of what makes a great business boss. It is better, in his opinion, to make a higher ratio of wrong decisions than to make a handful of correct decisions but leave lots of questions unanswered. At least if it's a wrong decision, you'll learn not to do it again and you'll grow as an entrepreneur.

"For me, 51 good decisions out of 100 is better than two out of three. Two in three is a better ratio, but with 51, you get more business done. So stop doing research, stop discussing the same old issues, decide and move. Make decisions, because at the end of the day you'll get something happening.

"A lot of junior people at a lot of big companies – well managed or not – are unable to take decisions, they always feel as though they have to report. Often it is because a blame culture exists and people are worried. It's definitely a challenge for companies to encourage decision-making."

Outsource if you can
Kanya King, MOBO Awards

As the MOBO brand grew, its founder Kanya King took on more and more staff to cope with the increasing demands of bigger and bolder events. She soon realised the shortcomings of hiring people full-time for an annual event and today most tasks are farmed out to contractors.

This option saved MOBO money and administration, and it meant that the business benefited from part-timers who are skilled in specific areas of event production. King says the decision made a huge amount of difference.

"I'm a great believer in working together and collaborating in a great partnership, because nobody gets anywhere alone and these guys are specialists. We used to do practically everything, but now we've streamlined our staff very well.

"Sometimes we end up with freelancers who are practically employed. Sometimes you work with the same people every year. We're good at keeping the balance right, not just having new people working in the organisation, but teaming old and new people up."

Consider your business model before you start
Kavita Oberoi, Oberoi Consulting

Starting up an advisory business is one of the cheapest options open to entrepreneurs, which is probably why there are so many consultants about. Kavita Oberoi believes the lack of overheads contributed greatly to the early success of her business.

"I was selling a service, so initially it was just my time and that helped me to build up the profits and invest in the people. I knew I had the work on offer. I was working from home so I didn't need offices and I didn't need to go and buy stock.

"The way I thought about it was if it doesn't work out, I can always go and get another job. I worked out that if I did consultancy, I'd only have to work about three days a month to get the same take-home pay I'd made in my previous job. If I couldn't sell this service then I knew I could sell something else as I'd acquired the right skills."

No amount of planning can prevent problems
Lord Bilimoria, Cobra Beer

Even the best laid plans go awry occasionally. A truism of business is that no amount of strategising can protect your business from the odd bump in the road. According to Lord Bilimoria, the mark of a successful entrepreneur is how you deal with those bumps, not whether you can avoid them.

"One of the keys to succeeding when growing a business is the ability to be adaptable and flexible, because what you can guarantee is that you're going to be surprised by events, quite often out of your control.

"They can happen by no fault of your own and it's how you deal with those events that determines whether you survive or not."

Just being green is not enough
Mark Constantine, Lush

If green is your game then beware. Although environmentally-friendly business are all the rage, you can't rely on green credentials alone to shift your stock. According to Mark Constantine of ethical shop chain Lush, consumers want quality and value for money first and foremost.

"Consumerism is by its nature not very environmental, but people are going to consume anyway, so my goal is to create something better than my competitors or produce things in a different way and set an example.

"The lovely thing about green business is that it shares a lot in common with best-practice business: cutting costs, cutting waste, lowering energy bills, reducing packaging, insulating buildings – all of those things have a positive impact on any bottom line.

"Generally people are more concerned – and quite rightly so – with what effect the product will have on them and whether it's value for money. After that they start looking at the green principles; most are initially coming in to our shops because they like the products."

Get everything right and you won't go wrong
Martha Lane Fox, Lastminute.com

Lastminute.com was the darling of the British dotcom boom. Unlike other high-profile internet ventures of the day it survived to tell the tale and remains a flourishing business. Co-founder Martha Lane Fox credits the product, PR and technology for the website's durability.

"Lastminute.com didn't go bust because it was a good idea – and I can say that because it wasn't my idea, it was [co-founder] Brent's; he just got me involved very early on. There were lots of other high-profile burnouts because the technology wasn't quite ready or they spent too much cash, or maybe the product wasn't right.

"We were lucky; we had a good idea, enough cash, lots of fabulous reasons for customers to come and use our website, the benefit of extraordinary PR people, and it was amazing how quickly we were taken into the public's conscience."

Keep your business small if you want to
Max Clifford, PR

Despite his stature in the media, Max Clifford never sought to grow his eponymous business into a large international firm. As he built a media profile and a reputation as the UK's number-one publicist, Clifford realised he could attract more than enough clients without hiring extra staff or renting bigger office space.

"It's always been a small businesses and I like to keep it that way. The overheads are small, there are only ten of us, but that's partly because I never planned to build an empire in terms of size, and secondly I need to be in the middle of everything – that works for me.

"It's worked very well from a business point of view too, for a small business we have worldwide attention and because of that I have never had to pitch for business, which I think is unique in this industry."

Build in some optimism
Peter Jones, *Dragons' Den*, Phones International

Peter Jones describes his approach to business as optimistic. He believes that start-ups should front-load confidence into their business plans. For him, entrepreneurs should express caution when it comes to cash-flow and growth projections, but that their calculations should come under an umbrella of unquestioning self-belief.

"Unfortunately, we have developed a little bit of a negative mindset in this country and we could do with a cultural shift. At the moment we think, 'Can I do it? Maybe. I'll give it a go.' It should be, 'I'm going to do this, I can do it.'

"I lost everything before I started Phones International and I had no other thoughts in my head than this is going to be a success. Having said that, because I had lost everything it was easy to have that mindset – things couldn't really get any worse."

Plans will always change
Rupert Clevely, Geronimo Inns

Most entrepreneurs agree it's vital to have a plan, whether written down or agreed verbally between the founders and senior management. But Rupert Clevely of Geronimo Inns argues that business plans must be flexible so that businesses can adapt to changes in the economy and other unforeseen events.

Exit plans are an important part of business too, because they mark out to shareholders and staff the ideal stage in the business' lifecycle at which it is to be sold. Again, says Clevely, a degree of flexibility is a must, even if that means offsetting retirement for two or three years.

"Always set out time lines when you go into these things and in a business where you've got external investors you need to be clear what your exit plan is.

"But you have to accept that if you say, 'I want to get from here to there in three years' time', then it might all work to plan, but the reality is that you've got to accept that it might be five years or more, or maybe less.

"Be flexible but have a goal."

Your plans should involve more than money
Simon Nixon, Moneysupermarket.com

Having made his fortune Simon Nixon's motivation for starting a business is different to most people's. His plans still involve making money, but he is a lot more interested in being right about his business hunches and turning his ideas into a major success.

"For me, success is not about how much money you make, it's how many people use your website and what benefit they derive from it.

"I don't mean just people looking at it but doing something with the site as well. That to me is the first level of success. Our aspirations are much higher than that, but that would be the first step, where we could say we've built something that's affecting lots of people's lives."

Aim to be number two
Sir Tom Farmer, Kwik-Fit

For Tom Farmer, aiming to be the best is all well and good, but for a start-up that goal is too much of a leap. His strategy was to aim to be second biggest, best and most profitable, and learn from the market leader. Once you have drawn all the inspiration you can from them, then make the push for first place.

"Aim to be second, first. Let them carve a path through the jungle and you can always follow. I spent a lot of my time going round other companies in other countries and asking how they do things. I had no problem with copying people; we made improvements and eventually we became the pioneers."

Planning is for wimps
Wayne Hemingway, Red or Dead

Red or Dead's strategy was not to have a strategy. Its co-founder Wayne Hemingway says he has never written a business plan in his life. Writing down what you want to do is only useful if you need to show it to a bank, he says.

"We didn't make loads of mistakes and therefore we were able to grow, so we never felt the need to plan out a course of action, and to this day we have never written down our strategy. When something is going wrong just stop doing it, but you must be close enough to your business to recognise those occasions."

Trust in macroeconomics
Dawn Gibbbins, Flowcrete

The inspiration for Dawn Gibbins' business, Barefoot Floors, came from statistics. When you're thinking about starting a business, it's a good idea to listen out for expert opinions and information on the future of industries and the buying power of groups you plan to target.

In Gibbins' case, she heard that the spending power of women is expected to increase in the near future so that soon the majority of buying decisions will be influenced by them. This, coupled with scientific research suggesting that walking barefoot is good for you, gave her the inspiration for her range of 'couture' floors.

"I went on a programme called *Filthy Rich and Female* and they were spouting stats about women being involved in 60% of purchases by 2025. There are so many up-and-coming women because the baby boomers are much more confident and educated and many have benefited [sic] from divorce payouts or inheriting money.

"So we looked at that and concluded that we needed to get into that market. I wondered how I could do this with flooring, then I started to look at the home market. Nobody's ever been into the home market with seamless flooring, so we're creating solutions for high-end housing and apartments."

RECESSIONS

Don't be ashamed to earn a living
Brad Burton, 4Networking

When 4Networking's Brad Burton ran out of money he swallowed his pride and took a job delivering pizzas to supplement his business. It's his firm belief that entrepreneurs should go through a period of financial hardship to give them context and teach them caution when business is booming.

He says too many entrepreneurs point their finger at prevailing economic circumstances as an excuse when they fail in business.

"It's too easy for people to use the recession as an excuse when actually the reason a lot of companies fail is because of terrible business practices. I should have been delivering pizzas eight months before I started. I resisted it to the detriment of me and my family. People are unwilling to do the things they need to do.

"If you're serious about your business then you do what it takes. It also puts life into perspective. When I was delivering pizzas, earning six pounds an hour, I thought about when I worked in Old Street and was spending eight quid on a bagel and a cup of coffee! Things change."

React to economic downturns before they happen
Dame Mary Perkins, Specsavers

For Dame Mary Perkins, anticipating a recession and dealing with it on a global scale was of paramount importance to her business, Specsavers. The joint-venture structure of the business means opticians all over the world look to the brand for protection in a downturn.

"We saw the 2008/09 credit crunch coming and we knew it was going to be a problem so we took steps to mitigate its impact. We expanded our value product range and we advertised the fact. We also introduced new offers.

"In addition we changed our marketing to tell people they can get really good value for money at Specsavers. What that achieved was to bring in lots of new customers who are all spending slightly less per person."

View your product in light of the economy
Deborah Meaden, *Dragons' Den*

According to Deborah Meaden, people planning to start a business should consider their product or service in light of prevailing economic conditions. What might sell well in the boom times could prove unattractive to your market when the economy takes a tumble.

"Consider your product or service in the context of the economic climate. People who start businesses often think about their products for a long time before they get going. The economy is changing quite fast and anyone who decided on a product six months ago and hasn't updated their plan since is doing the wrong thing.

"Think about your offering in the current climate because it might well be that it is perfect, it might be even better in this climate. It might be a better time, but it might be a worse time."

You meet your best customers in recessions
Ian Powell, PricewaterhouseCoopers

PricewaterhouseCoopers chairman, Ian Powell, says recessions present opportunities as well as threats. While business is slow at his company's corporate finance arm, the restructuring business is doing incredibly well. But more important for Powell is the partnerships PwC forges in a recession, which only strengthen in the boom years.

"A recession throws up opportunities. We have the biggest restructuring business in the world. It's a very good counter-cyclical business. Also our clients need help in a recession and we have so many who have been through a recession before. The relationship you establish in a difficult time is much more sustainable for the future. There's a lot more loyalty.

"We're not immune to downturns, though; we do a lot of corporate finance work for example, and the big deals aren't there during those times. But by focusing on other parts of the business we keep in pretty good shape."

Recessions aren't all bad
James Caan, *Dragons' Den*, Hamilton Bradshaw

Recessions mean different things to different businesses. For some they are a period of painful cutbacks and belt-tightening, for others they represent an opportunity to grow by acquiring struggling competitors. For James Caans' Hamilton Bradshaw, the 2008/09 recession was a mix of both scenarios.

His private-equity firm has investments in a range of businesses encompassing several industries. Investments in retail and construction were hit by the downturn, but in other sectors there were plenty of enticing opportunities.

"The business climate is very challenging, but from Hamilton Bradshaw's perspective it's a very exciting time in the cycle because we are in the business of buying businesses and that is all based on valuations and competition.

"In 2009 we found a limited amount of competition about, it's dropped significantly, and price is a factor of competition. It's supply and demand so prices come down considerably."

Competitions offer free PR in downturns

Peter Jones, *Dragons' Den*, Phones International

Peter Jones thinks entering your business into competitions and for awards is a great way of promoting it for free. Apart from any prizes you might win, coming in the top group of respectable businesses turns the spotlight on you and gives the business the sort of kudos that attracts new sales.

"Awards and competitions are important because in difficult economic times it's important to get your business out there in the market. You can go through PR companies, get them to shout about it and it doesn't cost anything. As an added benefit it forces you to focus on your own business plan; there's nothing to lose.

"It puts a magnifying glass over your business and gets it known in the wider community. Another great thing is that you have to pitch it to people who have spent many years investing in businesses or building them, so you get even more doors opening."

In a recession, focus on quality and cost

Rupert Clevely, Geronimo Inns

Rupert Clevely's business, Geronimo Inns, is a growing pub chain in London focusing on comfort, food and a diverse range of beverages. He believes it is the business' simplicity and commitment to quality that keeps it growing.

"We're very lucky; we weren't affected by the 2008/09 recession. In fact, we grew; we had a record period of sales in the business. But that's because we're largely in London, we have good sites, we offer good value for money and hopefully, when you try the food, you say, 'Wow, that was better than I was expecting in a pub'.

"I think that's the key and if we can continue to give our customers that, we'll be in a very good place going forward. If we can't, then we won't. For us, it's about good value. It's about fun, it's about being lively and buzzy. We're in a good spot and the business makes sense."

Don't let a downturn put you off
Simon Nixon, Moneysupermarket.com

Simon Nixon's view of recessions is that they are a mild encumbrance to growth and no more. They certainly shouldn't put off entrepreneurs with a good business idea. Those, he says, should start up whether the economy is booming or bottoming out.

"I don't think the downturn in the economy has had any impact, because if you build a business that ultimately is going to be successful and people are going to use it, a recession just means that it might be slightly less successful for a period of time."

Some business models flourish when the chips are down
Rob Shreeve, One Alfred Place

Rob Shreeve's One Alfred Place is another example of a business that made the most of a recession. He managed to grow the membership of the club and increase spend in his bar and restaurant even though generally people were tightening their purse strings.

His explanation is that the business people who use the club want to entertain clients in luxurious surroundings but don't necessarily want to fork out for their own expensive office space.

"People are eating and entertaining a lot more and ours is probably one of the few restaurants in the country that can say that we doubled our turnover in the six months when the credit crunch really hit hard.

"The logic of that, one assumes, is that people are working harder here – on the whole the membership of the club is entrepreneurs, small businesses, creative groups and the creative industry. If you want to impress clients you take them to lunch, you pitch, you take a boardroom, you do things in style. So in a demonstrable way, we've benefited."

SALES AND SELLING

Learn the art of sales

Anthony Ganjou, Curb

Before Anthony Ganjou set up Curb he gave himself a master class in sales. Straight out of university he joined an unusual American company which had a remit to sell just about anything. Soon Ganjou found himself leading a team of 17 people on the streets of London selling anything to anyone.

"Every day they gave me a tube map and a bag full of goodies like crayons, books and teddies and I would have to go to Tottenham Court Road and walk into every single club, shop or bar with the prices in my hand and pitch them to every person in that place. It was the rawest form of selling possible.

"It was an incredibly good learning exercise in terms of the real world and how you manage the stock and sell and market yourself. I was lucky enough and worked hard enough to build a team of 17 people during the course of about a year and a half and we were doing about £75,000 of sales a month.

"I learned more in the first six months than I learned in three years at university, because what that teaches you is the ability to connect instantly with someone. If you don't, you don't get anywhere and that's something I've taken into the business that I do now. Running a business is all about selling and without that, you don't really have anything."

Softly softly, catchee monkey

Ashley Ward, NEXEC Partners, Wharfedale, Orchestream

Ashley Ward started his career as a salesman and was taught a very heavy-handed sales technique, which involved backing the customer into a corner and 'forcing' them to buy. As Ward developed in his career he established his own approach which he feels works a lot better.

"I was trained in a very old-fashioned and aggressive sales method, which made people feel uncomfortable. Taking the keystone from that I developed a gentler approach, which I call intravenous salesmanship because it gets under customers' skin.

"It doesn't involve any pain, though; all I do is inform people about something that can help them. It's a very backed-off sell and it works very well. Sales should be all about communicating and building trust: you spot a genuine need and you suggest a way in which you can help."

Look for efficient ways to boost sales

Gerry Calabrese, The Hoxton Pony

Though still a relatively new business, Gerry Calabrese's Hoxton Pony already generates bar sales of up to £80,000 a week. He puts its early success down to the unusual design.

But more importantly for Calabrese is the back-bar layout which he himself designed for maximum efficiency. It saves him money on the wage bill because he needs fewer bartenders to serve drinks and it means his customers spend less of their evenings standing at the bar.

"I invested £75,000 in the back-bar systems alone and I practise something called 'one step bar-tending'. The idea is that the bartender has everything within his reach – within one step. A standard operator of our size would have 12 people serving. I have six.

"I try very hard to employ the right people and that, coupled with the system, really works. Everyone's got their own till, their own fridge and freezer and everything's within a hand's grasp. Everything's faster. The longest wait at the bar here for a cocktail is about eight to ten minutes. That is unheard of for a cocktail bar on a busy Friday or Saturday night."

Sell more than you spend

Gil Steyaert, Adidas

It sounds obvious, but when you start a business everything you do has a cost. Creating a product, researching the market, getting suppliers, finding a workspace, equipment and staff, all comes at a price.

For Gil Steyaert this is a reality that people must grasp, because cancelling out and then exceeding these costs with revenue is the fundamental point of being in business in the first place. How to earn more revenue than you have costs is a question that should be on an entrepreneur's mind day in, day out.

"When you start a business, whether it be investing in capital or investing in resource, you incur costs. You have to turn a profit at the end, so you have to build value. What makes value in a sustainable business is your unique selling proposition.

"You have to build value because everything has a cost and the profit will be made by what you generate. So you have to create superior value; it could be from your service to the consumer, your product innovation, the efficiency of operation, anything, but you have to build a competitive advantage."

Get the media to sell for you
Jennifer Irvine, The Pure Package

Jennifer Irvine used the media to great effect in gathering new sales when she founded her business, The Pure Package. Without employing the services of a PR or marketing agency she sourced all of her original clients through articles in newspapers and magazines.

"I was doing my initial preparation before I launched the company and I needed people to taste the food and give me feedback on all aspects of the service. I used to ask my friends to do it but they were too nice and would always say, 'This is fantastic, send me some more free food'.

"I started asking opinionated journalists. I picked people out of newspapers and magazines who seemed as though they had their heads screwed on and I contacted them and asked for their opinion; I wasn't looking for a piece, just to send them lots of free food.

"The problem was they had to fill in my nine-page questionnaire. But they were great and sent back lots of opinions and some of those journalists wrote pieces about us anyway. From those articles, I got my first clients."

Sometimes biting off more than you can chew is a good thing
Kavita Oberoi, Oberoi Consulting

Within a few months of Kavita Oberoi starting her consulting business, she landed a huge £500,000 contract through an introduction by a friend at a blue-chip pharmaceutical company. Having sold her services to the client, Oberoi's micro-business had to fulfil the giant contract.

"It did mean that I was working 24/7, literally going out and doing the delivery and other chores before coming back and running the rest of the business until I was able to get staff in place.

"It was exciting and stressful, but I knew it was something that I absolutely had to deliver. It was make or break so there was no option, but I'd set myself up to do that. I chose to go down that route, to take a chance and take on more work than I had ever coped with before. And I was pleased with the end result."

Start early
Keith Potts, Jobsite

Keith Potts, co-founder of recruitment portal Jobsite, started in business while he was still at school. Despite his tender age, the dotcom millionaire was able to conceive some sophisticated sales techniques which impressed his buddies.

"Since childhood I've always been quite interested in business. I remember renting out Top Trump cards to the other kids. I'd buy them with my pocket money on Saturday and instead of just using them myself I would rent them out at two pence a lunch break.

"Rather than having a toy and saying to somebody, 'Do you want to borrow this toy and give me some money?', I made it like a proper business. Before I started monetising it, I'd built up a range of these things from Top Trumps to little pinball machines and all the pocket games we used to have in the 70s."

Sales are not the same as profits
Mark Constantine, Lush

Mark Constantine turned Lush into a global high-street chain; he also experienced significant success with his first business, a cosmetics manufacturer which supplied The Body Shop. But in-between these blockbuster businesses he launched mail order firm, Cosmetics to Go, which flopped and cost him millions.

Constantine puts the failure down to a combination of bad timing (it launched as a recession occurred) and bad figures (the business lost money on every item sold). He says the main lesson drawn from the experience was that fabulous sales don't always translate into bumper profits.

"It wasn't profitable, we blew all the money and we went bust. We were selling in great volumes and every time we sold something we lost a quid. It was a nightmare really. We were shifting millions of units!

"We were trying to build this British mail-order company up to a certain level where it could make a profit, but as always with these things you don't allow for recessions or post strikes or horrendous things like that."

Price your product correctly
Mark Zaleski, DailyMotion

When Mark Zaleski took a senior role at research firm Nielsen he found that it was underselling its services. His legacy at the business was a proper pricing structure that fitted the benefits it delivered to clients. Although pricing your product correctly is a business basic, his sales strategy was met with stiff resistance.

"A lot of people involved saw selling as something that Del Boy does rather than 'what is the value I am creating for the client and given that how much should I charge?'.

"I re-engineered the client sales and service elements so we were more commercial. You mustn't be greedy, though; you're building a relationship and the big trick is to demonstrate value."

Focus on sales for the best results
Michelle Dewberry, *The Apprentice*, Chiconomise

Having founded fashion website Chiconomise.com, Michelle Dewberry soon realised that the business had drifted away from its core objective. At heart a money-saving website for girls, it had evolved into an online style magazine. With the attention off sales, which came from deals with retailers featured in the newsletter, the site risked dragging down cash flow.

Having identified the problem, the team set about emphasising deals, offers and smart ways to save money. They removed less relevant content from prime spots on the homepage and placed them into an archive. Dewberry says the focus is now 90% on sales and deals.

"It started as a newsletter and developed into a website which we were guilty of overcomplicating and we got carried away. We went off message.

"We're back to our core message: saving you money. Everything needs to come back to that one central point. Everything that's on there is key to saving you money, and if it's not, it's gone."

If your product has legs, let it run
Peter Jones, *Dragons' Den*, Phones International

When Peter Jones famously backed Reggae Reggae Sauce entrepreneur Levi Roots in an episode of *Dragons' Den,* he unwittingly started a phenomenon. So strong is the brand that it fanned out across the edible world, partnering with multinational food corporations and launching a series of products influenced by Caribbean cuisine.

Anticipating the scope of the brand, Jones made introductions to executives in the supermarket and food production markets and gave Reggae Reggae sauce its chance to become a mega-brand. Jones argues that strong products should be allowed to develop and not be stifled.

"We had an energetic guy who clearly had good products and we were able use our contacts to leverage what he had created. I've got a very good licensing guy who licensed the brand and the products across lots of different genres in a very calculating way so that they get maximum exposure.

"We are just driving the brand and the great thing is the product line is excellent, not just from the name but the product quality itself."

When the going gets tough, improvise
Keith Potts, Jobsite

As a consumer tool the internet was still in its early development during the mid 1990s when Keith Potts founded Jobsite. Educating recruiters as to the merits of putting job vacancies online was a hard task. So, like all good entrepreneurs, he improvised.

"We would go into a recruitment agency and tell them they should be putting vacancies on our website, and they would ask, 'What's a website?'. We also ran an internet service provider so we'd sell them modems and access to the internet too.

"In the later months in 1995 and '96 we used to give away modems, just to get people online. We'd get a subscription, plus we'd get them putting their vacancies onto our website. It was a hard sell initially because they hadn't heard of it and in those days there weren't many interesting sites to look at.

"NASA was one of the good ones, so to demonstrate our product, our job board, I had to show pictures of astronauts and launchers at the Kennedy Space Center. It was quite strange, but it worked."

Selling your business isn't game over

Dawn Gibbins, Flowcrete

Selling your business is not necessarily the happily-ever-after story you imagine it would be. Many entrepreneurs, including Flowcrete's Dawn Gibbins, continue to start new businesses well after the point at which they need not work ever again.

Believe it or not, having lots of money isn't always the root of all happiness and most entrepreneurs who retire early find themselves pulled back into entrepreneurial pursuits for the love of doing business and not because they need the money.

"I was possessed and obsessed when I sold the business; wanting to set up this new enterprise, wanting a change. However, a lot of other people who sold their businesses wanted to chill out and relax, but then they find they've got nothing to do.

"I had quite a few people ring me after I'd sold the business, asking 'Are you lonely?' because they don't feel important any more. You'd been wanted by all your staff, all your financiers, all your customers, respected by them and then suddenly nothing. I just jumped straight into a new business."

Other great business titles from
Harriman House

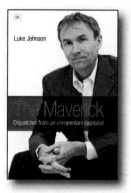

The Maverick
Dispatches from an
unrepentant capitalist
Luke Johnson

Taming the Lion
100 Secret Strategies for
Investing
Richard Farleigh

Start-up Smart
How to start and build
a business for £5000
Robin Bennett

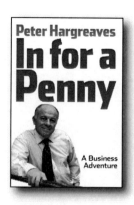

Eyewitness
The Inside Story of a
Publishing Phenomenon
Christopher Davis

In for a Penny
A Business Adventure
Peter Hargreaves

Managing Through
Turbulent Times
The 7 rules of crisis
management
Anthony Holmes

Hh Harriman House